International Relations in Action

A WORLD POLITICS SIMULATION

BROCK F. TESSMAN

LYNNE
RIENNER
PUBLISHERS

BOULDER
LONDON

To David Liebowitz, Stephen Lester, and my fantastic students
at the University of Denver and University of Colorado

Published in the United States of America in 2007 by
Lynne Rienner Publishers, Inc.
1800 30th Street, Boulder, Colorado 80301
www.rienner.com

and in the United Kingdom by
Lynne Rienner Publishers, Inc.
3 Henrietta Street, Covent Garden, London WC2E 8LU

Library of Congress Cataloging-in-Publication Data
Tessman, Brock, 1976–
    International relations in action : a world politics simulation / by Brock Tessman.
        p. cm.
    ISBN-13: 978-1-58826-464-0 (pbk. : alk. paper)
    ISBN-10: 1-58826-464-5 (pbk. : alk. paper)
    1. International relations—Study and teaching (Secondary)—Simulation methods.
2. Diplomacy—Study and teaching (Secondary)—Simulation methods. I. Title.
JZ1305.T44 2006
327.1071'2—dc22

                                                              2006030142

British Cataloguing in Publication Data
A Cataloguing in Publication record for this book
is available from the British Library.

Printed and bound in the United States of America

∞   The paper used in this publication meets the requirements
    of the American National Standard for Permanence of
    Paper for Printed Library Materials Z39.48-1992.

10 9 8 7

Contents

might also want to pursue the individual objective associated with your particular position.

The rest of this book follows a rather simple plan. In Part 1, you will be introduced to the individual position that you will occupy in your country's government, and the responsibilities that accompany each position. You will also learn about the tension that exists between individual and team objectives in the simulation. Finally, you will be given a crash course in the geography and history of each country in Politica. In Part 2, you will learn about the four basic components of each turn during the IRiA Simulation: allocation of resource factors, diplomacy, trade, and conflict. On every turn, you will have to make important decisions about challenges in the first three areas; occasionally, the fourth area—conflict—will also play an important role in your decisionmaking. Part 3 contains the twelve simulation scenarios that serve as the core of the IRiA Simulation. The scenarios are grouped into three broad categories of international security, international political economy, and international organization. Along with each scenario comes a new objective, but you will find that achieving one objective might require some compromise on another.

PART 1
Let the Games Begin

1 | Individual and Team Objectives

The position you occupy on your team will have a large impact on your objectives in the simulation. While all individual members are equally responsible for helping their team score objective points, there may be disagreement when it comes to deciding on the best strategy for doing so. There is an inherent tension in the simulation between the needs of the team and the needs of the individual leaders that comprise that team. It is up to you (and your teammates) to strike the right balance between those needs.

| Individual Positions and Objectives

It is important to emphasize that all positions are equally capable of engaging in all activities that occur during the IRiA Simulation. Anyone can get involved in planning, bargaining, and interaction with other simulation participants. That said, there may be some serious differences when it comes to the priorities of individual team members. These differences stem in large part from the distinct objectives that accompany each position. As mentioned, your team will have one or more of the following positions: chief decisionmaker (CDM), diplomat (DIP), economic adviser (ECA), intelligence officer (INT), and opposition leader (OPP). Depending on the size of your class, your country may operate without one or more of these positions, or it may be the case that your country has more than one member playing these roles. The following section discusses some of the key responsibilities and individual objectives of each position.

Chief Decisionmaker

The chief decisionmaker (CDM) serves as the head of state and must approve of any action taken by his or her country during the simulation. Because their approval is a necessary component of any action, the CDM is a key player on every team. As head of state, the CDM is chiefly concerned with matters of security. While economic prosperity is important and participation in global organizations can be beneficial, these issues are not given the same priority as are issues that relate to security. With this in mind, the individual objective of the CDM is to focus on scoring as many points as possible during the four international security scenarios. The CDM of the country that scores the most objective points in these scenarios will be considered the individual CDM winner.

Diplomat

The diplomat (DIP) functions as the foreign minister during the simulation. While the DIP does not have the same clout as the CDM (the DIP is not required to approve each and every decision made by the state), they should be an extremely active negotiator and should take pride in their role as the public face of their country. As foreign minister, the DIP is very concerned about matters related to cooperation with other states in Politica. Thus, the individual winner among all diplomats will be determined by the number of objective points each country achieves in the four international organization scenarios.

Economic Adviser

Economic advisers (ECAs) are charged with pursuing their country's material interests in Politica. As the ECA, you are convinced that prosperity generates security and that wealth fosters cooperation. Like all team members, the ECA will participate in all aspects of planning and negotiation, but the individual objective of the ECA is to score as many points as possible during the four international political economy scenarios. The ECA on the country that scores most points in these scenarios will be declared individual winner among economic advisers.

Intelligence Officer

The intelligence officer (INT) is continually focused on national security matters. The INT believes that economic prosperity and social welfare are worthless if a society is not protected. Over the course of the IRiA Simulation, each country has to make decisions about how they will allocate their finite resources. In general, resources can be spent on "guns" (security) or "butter" (economic growth). The INT is interested in convincing his or her teammates to allocate as many resources as possible to security. The individual INT winner will be determined by tallying the total resource factors each country spends on guns over the course of the simulation. The INT on the team that allocates the most factors to this area will be the winner.

Opposition Leader

The opposition leader (OPP) is the voice of the people. As such, the OPP is interested in convincing his or her team to allocate as many resources as possible to economic or social programs. In rough terms, these programs are supported when countries spend resource factors on butter rather than guns. Because each country has a finite number of resources, the OPP will often disagree with the INT when it comes to the distribution of resource factors during the simulation. The individual OPP winner will be determined by tallying the total resource factors each country spends on butter over the course of the simulation. The OPP on the team that allocates the most factors to this area will be the winner.

* * *

It is up to you to decide how much emphasis you will place on your individual objective. You may decide to place your country's objectives over your own; conversely, you might decide to forsake your team in hopes of being recognized as an individual standout. Your decision will be based on your personality, the chemistry your team has, or maybe even the way in which the simulation is unfolding. In this way, the IRiA Simulation mirrors the balance between individual and national interests that characterizes international politics.

| Team Objectives

Your country's primary goal is to earn objective points. Based on the particular position you occupy on your team, you might be more interested in achieving certain types of objectives than you are others. In each of the twelve scenarios that you will encounter during the simulation, there will be instructions that let you know what is necessary to score objective points during that scenario. Certain scenarios will be more important to you and your country than others. Scenarios fall into three broad categories: international security, international political economy, and international organization. There are four scenarios in each category. One scenario in each category will be worth 10 objective points for your country, one will be worth 5 points, one 3 points, and one scenario will only be worth a single objective point. Thus, it is likely that you will spend a lot of time and energy ensuring that your 10 point objectives are achieved; your 1 point objectives may not garner much attention at all. In some cases, it might make sense to compromise on a lower priority objective to score big on an important one. Use Table 1.1 to keep track of the objective points you have achieved in each scenario. The more objectives it achieves, the more points your country will score. The country that has the most objective points at the end of the simulation is deemed the leading power in Politica and is considered the winner.

Table 1.1 Tracking Your Objective Points

Country Name:

Scenario Title	Objective Points Possible	Objective Points Scored
Alliance politics		
Territorial disputes		
Nuclear proliferation		
Ethnic conflict		
Free trade vs. protectionism		
Natural resource politics		
Currency crises		
Foreign aid		
Global security organizations		
International criminal courts		
Collective action problems		
Environmental challenges		

2
History and Geography

Although anthropologists are still uncertain about the origins of civilization in Politica, there is widespread agreement on matters relating to more recent history and current geography. What follows is a geographic, economic, and political snapshot of each country in Politica. Along the way, you will find it helpful to reference Figure 2.1, which serves as a physical and political map of Politica. It is most important to understand what makes your own country unique, but a solid knowledge of the history and geography of others states will prove quite an asset as you progress through the IRiA Simulation.

Paxony

Paxony is a liberal democracy situated at the crossroads of Politica. Historical trade and migration routes almost always passed through what is today Paxon land; the result of which is a populous, ethnically diverse country that considers itself the birthplace and current hub of Politican civilization. Fishing is bountiful in the coastal waters of the North Placidic Sea, while significant mineral deposits are found in the Longa Mountains and Telon Highlands that dominate the west and north of the country. The winding path of the Kohridor River defines the southern and eastern borders of Paxony. Over the millennia, the river has carved out wide and fertile valleys that are currently the most productive agricultural areas in all of Politica. As the Kohridor River flows eastward, it splits into two branches; between these two branches exists a vast grassland ecosystem known as Centralia. This land is known for its historical susceptibility to invasion and its plentiful natural resources. As a result of a peace settlement that ended its victorious war against Industrael, control of Centralia was transferred from Industrael to Paxony. Successfully incorporating Centralia has

2.1 Map of Politica

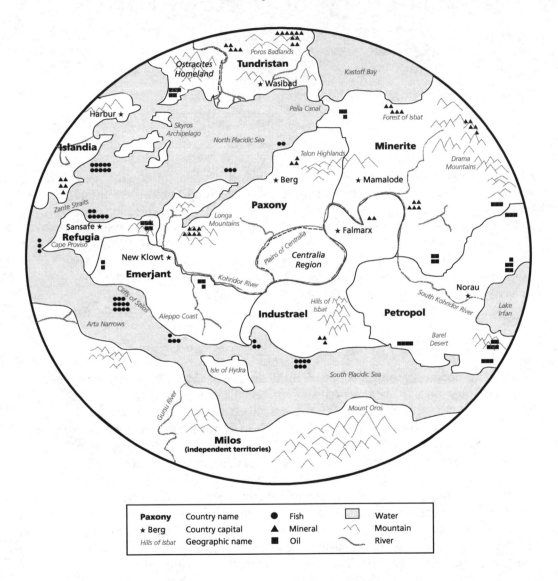

been quite difficult; there is increasing evidence of social resentment and economic decay among the region's inhabitants. In the broader world of Politican relations, Paxony is a pivotal state with a great deal of political, social, and diplomatic clout. It is, along with Industrael and Islandia, a permanent member of the prestigious Politican Security Forum (PSF). It is also one of Politica's two nuclear powers. Its capital city of Berg is arguably the center of all Politican politics. The PSF is headquartered in Berg and it hosts almost every important political meeting or economic summit in Politica.

Refugia

Refugia is a democratic country with a dearth of people but an abundance of resources. Most Refugees are Ostracites—an ancient ethnic group descended from early fishermen that sailed the waters of the North Placidic Sea. Other countries with a large population of Ostracites include Islandia and Tundristan. Much of Refugia is situated on the water, and the fishing industry still dominates economic and social life in the country. The waters off the northern and western coast provide a seemingly endless fish catch year after year, although over-fishing has begun to take its toll in particularly popular locations. The eastern half of Refugia is almost totally uninhabited, but there have been recent discoveries of oil deposits in the western end of the Longa Mountain Range. The Longa Range extends east into Paxony and the regional population has strong ties with their compatriots across the border.

Despite its small population and modest economy, the strategic importance of Refugia has never been questioned. Along with the country of Islandia, Refugia controls the narrow Zante Straits—the only navigable sea route between the North and South Placidic Seas. From a series of fortresses positioned at strategic points on Cape Proviso, Refugees have the ability to control the passage of all military and merchant ships through the straits. This power has long been a source of pride for Refugia, but it has also made Refugee territory a tempting target for larger countries that stand to suffer should Refugia decide—for whatever reason—to close the Zante Straits. Refugia has only closed the Straits twice in the past century and in both instances the Refugee capital of Sansafe was bombarded by Tundristan ships in protest. Full-scale war was narrowly averted, but relations between Refugia and Tundristan have been severely soured as a result of the confrontations. Refugia often complains about the treatment that the Ostracites receive in their semiautonomous homeland in western Tundristan. Refugia's only other rival in Politica is Petropol. There is a long history of ethnic conflict between Ostracites and ethnic Petropoleans. Recently, Petropol has made noise about developing an arsenal of nuclear weapons. This news has caused a great deal of anxiety in Refugia, with some radical leaders in Sansafe calling for Refugees to acquire their own nuclear deterrent.

Emerjant

Emerjant is low and flat, with extensive agricultural land just slightly above sea level along the famous Aleppo Coast. The highest points in all of Emerjant are the Cliffs of Stilos that jut abruptly from the South Placidic Sea along the western portion of the Emerjant shore. In the north, rolling plains host the capital city of New Klowt, and a rapidly growing industrial sector lines the southern banks of the Kohridor River. The climate is semitropical in the south, but the north of the country experiences the temperate climate of Paxony and Minerite. Recently, two minor oil fields were developed in Emerjant, which has allowed it to achieve a certain measure of energy self-sufficiency. Massive fishing resources are a blessing for the country. Its fishermen, though not as well known as the Ostracites in neighboring Refugia, actually bring home the largest annual catch in all of Politica.

Emerjant is governed by the relics of a military junta that has dominated politics for over fifty years. While there is a great deal of public resentment toward the authoritarian leadership, a booming economy has kept open protest to a minimum. As Emerjant looks toward the future, both its leaders and common citizens hope to join Industrael and Paxony in the ranks of the truly great powers in Politica. Indeed, the country has developed very close ties with Industrael and has even managed to maintain surprisingly decent relations with Industrael's chief rival Paxony. The only true enemy of Emerjant comes in the form of Tundristan. Ancient raiding parties from that northern land committed horrible atrocities in ancient Emerjant and only the sheer geographic distance between the two countries prevents open conflict.

Tundristan

Over one-third of the mountainous northern country of Tundristan is covered with ice fields and glaciers. Predictably, the climate is harsh and the growing season is short in such a land. Still, the harsh hills hold a bounty of vast mineral deposits. The pristine beauty of the tundra also lends itself to a healthy tourism industry in Tundristan. The capital city of Wasibad sits in the slightly warmer south, not far from the shores of the North Placidic Sea. This part of the country contains what little arable land there is in Tundristan, although the abbreviated growing season prevents widespread agriculture.

The unforgiving climate and a sparse population have hindered industrial growth in Tundristan. What industry there is has a hard time competing with imports from more advanced countries like Islandia and Paxony. Recently, economic development has been centered on the discovery of a new oil field in the semiautonomous western region of Tundristan that serves as the recognized homeland of the oft-persecuted Ostracite peoples. The Tundreks were lauded for creating a semiautonomous homeland for the Ostracites, but alleged repression and a dispute over oil rights have led to a great deal of tension between the ethnic Ostracites and ruling monarchy in Tundristan. This, in turn, has led to strained relations between Tundristan and other countries with a large Ostracite population, such as Refugia. Tundristan does share strong ties with Petropol and neighboring Minerite, to which it is connected by the narrow Pella Isthmus.

| Industrael

While its global dominance was once unquestioned, recent years have been tough on Industrael. Although a large population and powerful military (Industrael and Paxony are the only nuclear powers in Politica) still evoke a certain sense of respect from other states, the authoritarian government has failed to facilitate modernization, and it is clear that the days of Industraelite primacy are long gone. Industrael's current boundaries are largely defined by water. The Kohridor River separates Industrael from Paxony in the west and Minerite in the north. The calm waters of the Placidic Sea lay to the south. Mineral resources are found near the capital of Falmarx in the north, and near the Hills of Isbat in the south. Bountiful fishing waters have always kept the Industraelites well fed.

At one point in time, the Industraelite Empire encompassed modern-day Emerjant, Petropol, and the Centralia region of Paxony. Defeat in war and internal rebellion have led Industrael to slowly relinquish these territorial holdings, however, and today Industrael's boundaries are disparagingly described as looking like a melting hourglass. As is the case with most imperial powers, Industrael has plenty of enemies in Politica. A long-standing rivalry with Paxony has led to a number of devastating wars between the two countries. After defeat in the last such war, a peace settlement forced Industrael to transfer the resource-rich and industrially advanced region of Centralia to Paxony. This has been a source of grief for Industrael in the ensuing years, particularly after reports emerged that the large Industraelite population in Centralia was being persecuted by the ruling Paxons. Despite the persistence of rivalry with Paxony, relations with neighbors Emerjant and Petropol have warmed significantly in recent times as those countries attempt to balance the growing power of Paxony and its allies.

Islandia

Islandia lies off the western coast of the Politican mainland. The bulk of its land is somewhat mountainous and unsuitable for agriculture; what arable land there is has been cultivated with the great efficiency that defines Islandish culture in general. Islandia is composed of four islands: the main island of Islandia and the three smaller islands of the Skyros Archipelago. These three smaller islands have been controlled by Islandia for centuries, but their rocky soil and wind-swept coastlines have made them unattractive for human settlement. The main island is home to the third largest national population in Politica. The capital city of Harbur is the largest human settlement north of the Kohridor River (the sprawling Petropolean metropolis of Norau is slightly larger). South of Harbur, extensive mineral deposits were exported in large amounts to fuel early development in Islandia.

Today, Islandia is the most technologically advanced society in Politica. Harbur serves as a key financial center for northern economies like Paxony and Minerite. Islandish factories produce almost half of the computer hardware and software in the world. The presence of a large Ostracite population has also kept Islandia tied closely to other states with sizeable Ostracite populations, such as Refugia and Tundristan. Because it depends so much on export-oriented growth, Islandia has aggressively pursued close relations with a wide range of trading partners, sometimes overlooking any political differences that may exist. The country has an imperial past, but has long been a stable and influential democracy. Islandia occupies, along with Industrael and Paxony, a permanent seat on the prestigious Politican Security Forum (PSF).

Petropol

Petropol occupies the southeastern portion of the Politican mainland. Most of the country is inhospitable to humans. The vast Barel Desert has average daily temperatures well in excess of 90 degrees Fahrenheit for most of the year. Most humans in Petropol have settled within a dozen miles of the southern branch of the Kohridor River, which flows from the northwest into Lake Irfan in the east. The expansive Petropolean capital of Norau sits right on the Kohridor and is currently the largest human settlement in Politica. The city is dominated by endless shantytowns—poverty is widespread in Petropol even though the country's elite enjoy a standard of living equal to that enjoyed by their counterparts in Paxony or Islandia. Petropol is governed by theocracy, and fundamental religiosity dominates daily life in this country. There has been a great deal of resistance to what Petropolean leaders have deemed the cultural depravity of states such as Minerite, Paxony, and Refugia.

This elite's high standard of living is supported by Petropol's tremendous oil reserves. A full 40 percent of Politica's oil originates in Petropol. Despite lacking any other natural resource wealth, Petropol's oil possessions alone have made the country a cherished trading partner for energy-hungry countries such as Industrael, Paxony, and Islandia. On a number of occasions, foreign governments have accused the Petropolean theocracy of intolerable political repression, only to have these accusations disappear when a reduction in oil supply is threatened. Recently, there have been rumors that Petropol is working on the development of an arsenal of nuclear weapons. Refugia has led the charge to keep Petropol from acquiring any nuclear capability, which is not surprising when one accounts for the deep animosity and history of violence between ethnic Petropoleans and the Ostracites that inhabit Refugia. The rest of Politica has a vested interest in Petropol's alleged nuclear gambit; with both nuclear weapons and almost half of Politica's oil reserves, Petropol would have unmatched political and economic clout.

| Minerite

Many onlookers have pegged Minerite as an emerging superpower. With a landmass that spans all the way from the northern ice fields near the Kastoff Bay to the intense heat near the Petropolean border, Minerite is the largest country in Politica. Economic development has taken off after the discovery of oil near the southern border with Petropol. In the mountains that dominate the far northern and eastern portions of Minerite, vast mineral deposits have served as a nice source of export income. Most industrial production in Minerite takes place near the capital of Mamalode. This city—called by many the most beautiful in Politica—is a cultural center beyond compare. All the best Politican artists, philosophers, and university students converge on Mamalode to mingle with like-minded counterparts.

As a prosperous and stable democracy, Minerite is truly a melting pot for all Politicans. The country has particularly close ties with its neighbor Paxony. With the decline of Industrael, Minerite wants to join Paxony as a leading power in Politica. As a first step, and as a symbol of its growing economic and cultural importance, Minerite has pushed for a permanent seat on the prestigious Politican Security Forum (currently permanent seats are reserved only for Industrael, Paxony, and Islandia). Minerite's southern neighbor Petropol has also shown interest in joining the PSF as a permanent member. A brewing competition between Petropol and Minerite would not only signal a potential changing of the guard in Politican politics, but would also highlight what appears to be a growing divide between the northern and southern states in the system.

PART 2
Basic Components
of the Simulation

On each turn of the simulation, you will need to make decisions in three crucial areas: allocation of resource factors, diplomacy, and trade. On some turns, you may also have to make decisions about getting involved in armed conflict. In the following section, you will learn about each of these areas—what terms and concepts are important to remember, what actions your country is required to take, and what rules you must abide by. Your instructor will let you know exactly how turns will be organized and what time frame you have to accomplish what is needed on each turn.

3

Resource Factors

In Politica, resource factors are synonymous with power. Factors can be used to build up your military strength or to promote overall prosperity. Factors can also be effective for achieving more specific objectives such as distribution of foreign aid or the completion of a massive public-works project. In general, countries with a large number of factors have more options available to them; they also enjoy a great deal of leverage in negotiations or conflict with weaker states. Not all countries in Politica start the simulation with the same factor allocation. Furthermore, a country's actions during the simulation are likely to result in a factor allocation that changes from one turn to another.

Initial Factor Allocations

To represent variation in relative power among different actors in Politica, some countries start the simulation with more factors than others. The two strongest states begin with 1,000 factors, while the two weakest countries are initially allocated 400 factors. Table 3.1 indicates the initial factor allocations for each of the eight countries in Politica.

Both Paxony and Industrael are economic and military giants in Politica; they start with the maximum allocation of 1,000 factors. On the other end of the spectrum, tiny Refugia and isolated Tundristan have 400. Islandia, Minerite, Emerjant, and Petropol are considered midrange powers and start the simulation with 600 to 800 factors.

Distributing Factors: Guns, Butter, and Action

Factors can be used to bolster military strength (guns), promote economic prosperity (butter), or to accomplish something specific (action). At the beginning of each

Table 3.1 Initial Factor Allocations

Country Name	Initial Factor Allocation
Paxony	1,000
Refugia	400
Emerjant	600
Tundristan	400
Industrael	1,000
Islandia	800
Petropol	600
Minerite	800

turn, countries must decide how many factors (if any) to spend in each area. Important choices about distribution have to be made, as no single factor can be used in more than one way. Depending on a country's immediate priorities, it may make sense to distribute factors equally among the three areas or it may be wise to invest more factors in one area at the expense of the other two. Decisions about distribution must be made at the beginning of each turn, so careful calculations are necessary to make sure that, as the turn progresses, factors are available for the specific objectives a country hopes to achieve. It is also prudent to engage in long-term planning because the manner in which a country distributes its factors on one turn directly determines its factor allocation on the next turn.

Guns

Factors spent in this area promote military strength. On any given turn, the strength of a country's armed forces is defined by the *total* number of factors it has spent on guns up to that point in the simulation. For example, if Petropol has spent 50 factors on guns during the first three turns, it has a military strength of 150 factors at that point in the simulation. Should Petropol find itself at war during that third turn, it could use up to all 150 factors in the conflict. By distributing spending factors on guns over the course of the game, a country can build up a great deal of military clout. These factors, however, do not contribute to an increased factor allocation on upcoming turns. Also, once they are used in conflict (regardless of the outcome), factors spent on guns are lost. Thus, a large military may be important to ensure national security, but overspending on guns might inhibit economic growth and actually limit the long-term military potential of the country in question. Depending on the strategic imperatives of a country, it may be the case that heavy spending on guns is counterproductive. In such a case, consistent investment in butter may be much more beneficial.

Butter

If factors devoted to guns are meant to broadly represent investment in military power, then factors spent on butter are considered to be directed toward industrial expansion, social programs, and other directions that promote overall prosperity. Factors that are invested in butter help to increase future factor allocations. They do not provide military security or battlefield strength, but investment in overall prosperity today could very well allow for higher spending on guns later in the simulation. Countries that do not feel threatened and do not plan aggressive action in the foreseeable future are thus well served by distributing a large number of factors to butter.

Action

Guns and butter spending is meant to symbolize general investment in the military and economic sectors, respectively. Action factors, however, are used for specific projects or expenditures. They do not contribute to military strength or help to increase upcoming factor allocations, but action factors are sometimes necessary because an objective requires that a number of factors be spent in a particular way. If Minerite was required to spend 400 factors on a giant statue to achieve a certain objective, it would have to first distribute the 400 factors to "action" and then file an action report that outlined exactly what the 400 factors were being applied to. Action factors can also be donated to other countries (as foreign aid) to use on future turns, given that the requisite action report is completed. Any unused action factors are lost at the end of the turn. With this in mind, countries should not earmark a large number of factors for action if there is not a strong possibility that those factors will be put to use on the current turn.

Factor Growth and Decline

Use Table 3.2 to keep track of your country's factor distribution on each turn and to calculate your factor allocation for the next turn. You can reference Table 3.1 in order to determine your country's initial factor allocation. After your country has decided how it will distribute its factors among guns, butter, and action, fill in the appropriate columns and be sure to check that the total distribution matches the initial allocation. In order to determine your country's next allocation, multiply the number of factors devoted to butter by 1.5. Then subtract any trade penalties (described in Chapter 5) that might apply. Be sure to also keep track of cumulative military strength by summing the total number of factors spent on guns on all turns up to the current one, subtracting any that were actually used in conflict with another country.

As an illustration, consider a hypothetical example involving the country of Tundristan: Tundristan starts the simulation with 400 factors. On the first turn, Tundristan spends 50 on guns, 300 on butter, and 50 on action. During the course of the turn, neither the guns nor action factors are used. To determine Tundristan's factor allocation for the next turn, simply multiply the 300 factors devoted to butter by 1.5 for a result of 450 factors. Tundristan was able to secure at least 5 units of oil, fish, and minerals, so no trade penalty is applied on this turn. The 50 factors spent on guns are entered into the military strength column at the far right of the table, while the 50 unused action factors are unfortunately lost. Table 3.3 illustrates this example using the factor worksheet provided in Table 3.2.

Table 3.2 Factor Distribution Worksheet

Country Name:

Turn No.	Starting Allocation	Guns	Butter	Action	Growth (Butter * 1.5)	Trade Penalty?	Next	Military Strength

Table 3.3 Factor Distribution Worksheet: An Example

Country Name: Tundristan

Turn No.	Starting Allocation	Guns	Butter	Action	Growth (Butter * 1.5)	Trade Penalty?	Next	Military Strength
1	400	50	300	50	450	0	450	50
2	450							

4

Diplomacy

Diplomacy functions as the heart of the IRiA Simulation. While some objectives simply require different states in Politica to work toward a common objective, other objectives might not be possible without at least some compromise. Still other objectives might be difficult to accomplish without experiencing at least some conflict. Thus, knowing when to compromise, threaten, and accommodate is crucial to success in the simulation. Countries will need to employ all three strategies in order to maximize the objective points they achieve. It is important to remember that—at least in this simulation—a country cannot always get what it wants, but if it acts prudently it can get most of what it wants most of the time.

Diplomatic Interaction

Although there are varying definitions of the term, diplomacy typically refers to the practice of negotiations between formally recognized representatives of any number of actors in a given system. As a recognized representative of a country in Politica, your interaction with other representatives is very much in the spirit of diplomacy. The nature of this interaction will change as you move from one simulation scenario to another. On one turn you may be lobbying another state for more development aid only to sanction that same state for pursuing nuclear weapons on the following turn. Throughout the simulation, your basic objective remains the same: Use the tools at your disposal (e.g., economic leverage, international legitimacy, the threat of force) to sway diplomatic outcomes in your favor.

Depending on the specific structure of your simulation, diplomatic interaction can occur in many different settings: at designated times in the classroom, via e-mail and instant messenger, or during meetings outside of class. Diplomacy might lead to heated negotiations over certain matters or a strong feeling of trust between countries that have found room for compromise or cooperation. In the end, it is up to the teams and individuals engaging in the simulation to decide the character of their interaction.

Domestic Politics

Remember that negotiation and compromise will occasionally be necessary between leaders from the same country. While they may share a common interest in achieving country objective points, each leader also has a personal interest in their individual objective as well. A country must prioritize the way it allocates time and resources and this can lead to some tension between different members of the same team. For example, a chief decisionmaker (CDM) may want to emphasize the importance of achieving as many objective points as possible in the international security scenarios while the economic adviser (ECA) is more likely to push for increased attention to the international political economy scenarios. Disagreement might also occur between the intelligence officer (INT) and the opposition leader (OPP) when it comes to spending on guns or butter. Most of the time, this kind of prioritizing involves the same kind of compromise that is required in diplomacy between countries. In general, the IRiA Simulation requires participants to balance loyalty to their country with their personal interests.

Country Action Reports

When (and if) internal compromise is achieved and a country wants to take action during the simulation, it must file a Country Action Report (CAR). These reports serve as the official record of events during the IRiA Simulation. No matter how obvious or well known a decision might appear *it does not become official until a signed and completed CAR is submitted*. Absolutely any announcement, agreement, or operation (broadly labeled "actions") that a country wants to formalize must be accompanied by a report. Figure 4.1 is a sample CAR that is completed to depict a hypothetical scenario in which Industrael, Paxony, and Islandia have agreed to send 400 factors of foreign aid to Tundristan. First, these four countries must all be listed under "relevant countries" found at the top of the action report. After this is done, the relevant countries need to agree on the specifics of the action to be taken. It is incredibly important to put a great deal of thought into this part of the CAR because whatever is written on the report will be considered part of the official record. The specific language used in the CAR will vary; a report that outlines a trade agreement between states will contain different information than a CAR that serves as a declaration of war. In the example above, Industrael, Paxony, and Islandia are sending foreign aid to Tundristan.

Figure 4.1 Sample Country Action Report

■ Relevant Countries (list all that are involved in action):

1. Paxony   5.

2. Industrael   6.

3. Islandia   7.

4. Tundristan   8.

■ Nature of Action (what are these countries agreeing to do?):

Paxony, Industrael, and Islandia agree to send 400 factors to Tundristan in the form of foreign aid.

200 factors will be sent by Industrael, while Paxony and Islandia will send 100 factors each. The aid will be sent this turn (drawn from the donor states' action factors) and will be available for Tundristan to use on the next turn.

It is agreed that this aid is earmarked for use in the Ostracite homeland in Tundristan. The aid is also considered a grant. As long as the 400 factors are used in the manner outlined in this report, Tundristan will not have to repay them to the donor countries.

■ Required Signatures (majority, including CDM, for democracies; CDM only for others):

	CDM	DIP	ECA	INT	OPP
Paxony	signature 1		signature 2	signature 3	
Refugia					
Emerjant					
Tundristan	signature 1				
Industrael	signature 1				
Islandia	signature 1	signature 2		signature 3	
Petropol					
Minerite					

When describing the nature of this action, it would be important to describe the total amount of aid being sent (400 factors), the amount being sent by each country (Industrael will send 200 factors, while Paxony and Islandia will send 100 factors each), the timing of the aid (it will be sent this turn and available for Tundristan to use next turn) and any qualifications that are part of the agreement (such as the conditions under which the aid will or will not need to be paid back to the lending countries). In general, the format of the CAR demands a clear, concise—*yet thorough*—description of the action in question. At the bottom of the report, each of the relevant countries must endorse the final copy of the CAR with a required number and type of signatures.

▌ Government Type and Required Signatures

Democracies (regardless of type) require a certain amount of domestic support in order to take actions during the IRiA Simulation. Paxony, Refugia, Islandia, and Minerite are considered to be democracies. Any action report filed by one of these countries must have the signed support of at least half the members from that country. One of the signatures must be that of the CDM. Thus, if a democracy like Paxony (with a full slate of five leaders) wants to send foreign aid to Tundristan as described in the earlier example, the CAR must be signed by the Paxon CDM and at least two more individuals from that country.

Nondemocracies (regardless of type) do not have the same requirement when it comes to signing action reports. To reflect the more centralized nature of decisionmaking in monarchies, theocracies, and dictatorships, actions only need to be supported by the CDM in order to be considered official. In the foreign aid example mentioned above, Tundristan (a monarchy) need only have its CDM sign in order to be officially included in the CAR. Identical rules apply to Industrael (a dictatorship). The other two relevant countries on the sample CAR (both democracies) require signatures from at least half of their members, one of which must be the CDM.

If one or more countries do not have the appropriate signatures, they are not officially included in the report. In some cases, this may alter the impact of a CAR. Imagine a CAR that outlined an alliance between Petropol and Emerjant. If Emerjant does not appropriately sign that report, then clearly an alliance between those two states cannot exist. In other instances, the action described in the CAR may be possible even with the omission of one or more countries. In the foreign aid example from earlier in this chapter, a lack of signatures from Paxony would prevent their portion of the aid (100 factors) from being sent to Tundristan, but the aid from Industrael (200 factors) and Islandia (100 factors) would still be sent.

5

Trade

Countries in Politica must have access to natural resources in order to satisfy economic, social, and military requirements. In this simulation, there are three kinds of natural resources: oil, fish, and minerals. Resources are found in the mountains, plains, deserts, and oceans of Politica. Reference Figure 2.1 (Map of Politica) for a basic idea of where certain resources are located. Oil resources are slightly scarcer than are fish and minerals; there are 45 units of the oil, and 50 units each of both fish and minerals. The eight countries of Politica each control a portion of this total resource pool. Table 5.1 lists the specific resources controlled by each state.

Resource Trading in Politica

In order to function properly, states must end each turn with at least 5 units of each resource. Several countries already possess 5 units of a particular resource. This means they do not need to trade in order to satisfy the requirement for that resource. Some states, however, start each turn with either greater or fewer than 5 units of one or more resources. A perfect example is Petropol. It is plentiful in oil (with 20 of the 45 total units) but lacks any access at all to either fish or minerals. In order to meet the requirement for fish and minerals, Petropol must acquire at least 5 units of both. Thus, it may make sense for Petropol to exchange or sell up to 15 units of oil (remember it should retain at least 5 units for itself) in order to gain access to at least 5 units of fish and minerals.

Because of the natural resource distribution in Politica, all countries must engage in at least some trade in order to gain access to the bare minimum of 5 units for each resource. Petropol could send 5 units of oil to Industrael in exchange for 10 units of fish. Petropol could then send 5 of its remaining 15 oil

Table 5.1 Natural Resources (listed by controlling country)

Country	Oil	Fish	Minerals	Total
Paxony	0	5	10	15
Refugia	5	10	0	15
Emerjant	5	15	0	20
Tundristan	5	0	15	20
Industrael	0	10	5	15
Islandia	0	10	5	15
Petropol	20	0	0	20
Minerite	10	0	15	25
Total	45	50	50	145

units to Paxony in return for 5 mineral units. With 10 oil units left and no further natural resource needs, Petropol could sell 5 units to another country in search of oil (Islandia in this scenario) for whatever number of factors the two sides agree upon. Islandia would draw those factors from their action sector and give them to Petropol for use on Petropol's next turn.

There is no direct incentive to end a turn with more than 5 units of any one resource: Resources do not carry over from one turn to the next—countries begin every turn with the resources listed in Table 5.1. Furthermore, there is no bonus of any kind for ending a turn with more than 5 units of any one factor. In some cases it may be difficult to convince a country to part with a particularly scarce resource, even if that country has a surplus as the turn comes to an end. That country may decide not to trade or sell that resource if the compensation is deemed less than satisfactory.

Penalties for Natural Resource Deficiency

If a country ends any turn with fewer than 5 units of any resource, a penalty of 50 factors is enforced in order to represent the economic, social, and military damage incurred as a result of the shortage. This penalty is enforced on the following turn. For each natural resource in which a country is lacking (i.e., possessing fewer than 5 units), 50 factors are subtracted from what would otherwise be that country's factor allocation. If Minerite had spent 800 factors on butter during the previous turn and had met the 5-unit requirement for each natural resource, its next factor allocation would be 1,200. If Minerite did not secure enough fish to meet the 5-unit requirement, however, a 50-point trade penalty would be enforced and its next factor allocation would be reduced to 1,150. Although sufficient access to natural resources is not necessary in order to achieve any specific objective points, it should be clear that natural resources are crucial to long-term growth.

There are no formal rules for conducting trade; states can exchange one type of resource for another or they can buy or sell resources for factors. If natural resources are purchased with factors, the factors must be drawn from the action sector. Countries that anticipate a need for purchasing natural resources should then be sure to distribute a sufficient number of factors to action at the beginning of the turn. Countries that sell natural resources for factors will have those factors available at the beginning of the following turn. All exchange rates and selling prices are determined through the bargaining process: It may very well be the case that one unit of a high demand resource is exchanged for two or more units of a more plentiful resource. In order to formalize any trade agreement (purchase or exchange), countries are required to submit an action report that outlines the nature of the trade and is signed by the relevant countries. Use Table 5.2 in order to keep track of your natural resources from turn to turn.

Table 5.2 Natural Resources Trading

Turn	Oil		Fish		Minerals		Penalty			Factors Penalized
	start	finish	start	finish	start	finish	oil	fish	minerals	

6
Conflict

One of the primary goals of the IRiA Simulation is to encourage teams and individuals to engage in bargaining, negotiation, and—to some extent—compromise. These processes constitute the bulk of international interactions in today's world. It is possible, however, that diplomacy alone will occasionally fail to resolve a dispute between countries. In such cases, one or more countries has the option of declaring war against one or more targets of that country's choosing. In this chapter, you will learn what can and cannot be achieved through armed conflict, the formal procedure for declaring war, and the way victory is determined.

| War: What Is It Good For? Some Things but Not Others

The most efficient way to achieve an objective in the IRiA Simulation is to convince other countries to do what you want them to do without resorting to war. Regardless of the outcome, the costs of war are high; among other things, factors are permanently lost and a country's reputation can be tarnished. There are some situations, however, in which a declaration of war is really the best option. An unpopular or exceedingly dangerous state may be so provocative that war is really the only way that the international community (or a portion of it) can constrain it. Two rivals may be so unwilling to compromise during an important scenario that the price of conflict seems acceptable to at least one country. Or, one side's preparation for war may be so obvious that the likely target decides to act preemptively.

In a hypothetical scenario, imagine that Tundristan has a 10 point objective that requires Minerite to join them in declaring that the Pella Canal (located right between the two countries) is closed to all foreign shipping traffic. If Tundristan's persistent and various diplomatic efforts are met with one Minerite refusal after another, then Tundrek leaders could decide that coercion is the only way to achieve the objective in question. If this decision is made, then a declaration of war might be an appealing strategy. Depending on the outcome of the war, however, such a strategy is no more likely to look like a stroke of genius than it is a bone-headed mistake.

Importantly, there is no mechanism for "total war" as defined by the goal of eliminating another country from the simulation. Aggressor countries that sign a declaration of war must confine their war aims to the boundaries of the current turn. Thus, based on the scenario(s) that are being addressed on the relevant turn, aggressor states are limited in what they can hope to achieve through conflict. Given these rules it should be clear that the outcome of any war is not retroactive; victory on turn four does not allow a country to change any agreements or events that took place on the first turn.

| Declaring War: Procedures and Guidelines

Once one or more countries decide to declare war on one or more other countries, a specific set of procedures must be followed. The first requirement is that the aggressor(s) signs an action report that includes the following items:

- The country (or countries) that is declaring war.
- The target or targets of this declaration.
- The war aims of the aggressor country or countries.
- The number of guns factors each aggressor is devoting to the war.

The completed action report will serve as the official declaration of war. *A declaration of war is submitted before the end of the current turn.* If the end of the turn is marked by the end of class, your instructor will require declarations of war to be submitted with a certain amount of time remaining in the class period. If the end of the turn is not marked by the end of class (which may be the case if the simulation is largely or entirely conducted online), your instructor will determine an appropriate deadline for declarations of war to be submitted. All aspects of the declaration will immediately be made public, with the exception of the number of guns factors that the aggressor(s) have devoted to the war. This will only be known after the current turn is over. Thus, even though the identity of the aggressor(s) is known to the defender(s), they do not know the exact number of guns factors that will be necessary to achieve victory in the war.

After a declaration of war is announced, the target(s) of the declaration will have the chance to solicit help in their defensive effort. Between the deadline for submission and the end of the current turn, defender(s) will need to complete and submit an action report that includes the following:

- The intention of the defender(s) to resist or surrender.
- If resisting, the war aims of the defender(s).
- If resisting, the number of guns factors each defender is devoting to the war.

The deadline for defender(s) to turn in their action report is defined by the end of the current turn. If an action report is not submitted, the target(s) of the declaration of war is assumed to surrender and the aggressor(s) achieves its war aims and half of any guns factors earmarked for war are returned to each aggressor. If, however, the defender(s) chooses to resist, the outcome of the conflict is determined by comparing the number of guns factors each side has spent on the war effort.

| Determining the Outcome of Conflict

In order to achieve the war aims they have identified, aggressor(s) must devote twice as many factors to the war effort as the defender(s) that aggressor has targeted. While this is certainly an advantage for the defender(s), remember that the aggressor(s) has the benefit of planning; the aggressor knows the time and place of the attack and also has more time to convince additional countries to join in the declaration of war. Conflict is settled through the use of a bidding system that allows states to commit some or all of their military strength to the war in question. Because neither side is aware of the factors spent by the other (remember that this part of the initial declaration of war is not made public), armed conflict is settled by using a blind bidding system. Both sides are aware of each other's basic military strength, but it is not always obvious how much of that strength has been devoted to the current conflict. Because of this uncertainty, it may be the case that the winning side "overpays" for victory. This is another potential cost of war in international politics.

After the outcome of the war is determined, the war aims of the victorious side are considered to be achieved. Outcomes that are achieved through war take precedence over any other action reports that were handed in at the end of the turn. If—from the example earlier in this chapter—Tundristan achieves its war aim and forces Minerite to join it in declaring the Pella Canal as off limits to foreign shipping, this outcome would be enforced even if Minerite had submitted an action report stating otherwise.

PART 3
The Simulation Scenarios

This section serves as the heart and soul of the IRiA Simulation. Twelve scenarios are presented in three broad categories: international security, international political economy, and international organization. There are four scenarios in each category, each with its own title, background, and country objectives. After reading about each scenario, you should be familiar with the basics of the scenario, what positions each country has taken, and how many objective points are at stake for you and your competitors. From this point, the next step is to formulate a successful strategy and begin negotiating with other countries. Remember that certain scenarios will be more important for your country than others, so focus your time and energy on maximizing your objective point total. To finalize any action, formalize any declaration, or take any official stance whatsoever, remember that it is necessary to fill out an action report. Action reports are the official record of events during the simulation. In most scenarios, you have to fill out an action report to score objective points.

In addition to the scenario background and country objectives, each of the following twelve chapters also includes: a Country Action Report, space for diplomatic notes, and an assessment worksheet you will need to fill out at the end of the scenario. You will also find a "For Further Review" capsule in each chapter. This capsule will provide contemporary and classic sources for more information on issues relating to the current scenario.

7

Alliance Politics

Trouble is brewing in Politica. A system long defined by a loose collection of strong and independent powers is showing signs of devolution into two competing, heavily armed camps: the North Placidic Treaty Organization (NPTO) and the New Politican Bloc (NPB). These alliance organizations have been promoted by two rising powers in Politica: Minerite and Emerjant. The NPTO is led by Minerite and based in their great city of Mamalode. As its name would suggest, the NPTO has mainly attracted attention from northern states that border the North Placidic Sea, such as Tundristan, Paxony, Refugia, and Islandia. Minerite has maintained that a coalition of northern states is vital as a protective measure against aggressive states like Industrael and quickly growing powers like Emerjant and Petropol. The NPB—formed just two short months after Minerite announced its intention to solicit membership in the NPTO—is based in the Emerjant city of New Klowt. Emerjant maintains that the NPB is only necessary because southern states feel a need for protection given the overwhelming strength of the states Minerite is trying to include in the NPTO.

Some states are supportive of Minerite and Emerjant and the initiative they have shown in attempting to form and lead protective alliances. Tundristan and Industrael have both shown a great deal of interest in joining the NPTO and the NPB, respectively. But other states have questioned the motivation that has guided recent Minerite and Emerjant behavior. Paxony and Petropol both feel that the diplomatic bravado displayed by both Minerite and Emerjant is part of a conscious strategy to assert themselves as the new political giants of Politica. Thus, Politican countries are faced with a decision: either join one of the two alliances in the name of protection or abstain from membership in an attempt to stay out of any trouble that might emerge as a result of armed confrontation. In the end, important questions must be answered: Do alliances offer shelter in a potential storm of conflict, or is nonalignment the only way to avoid fighting? If alliances do offer protection, which of the two blocs in Politica is more attractive to a prospective member?

For Further Review: Alliance Politics

Will the emergence of a powerful China cause a reshuffling of the international alliance system? *See* Zheng Bijian, "China's Rise to Great Power Status," *Foreign Affairs* 84, no. 5 (2005): 18–25.

Why do alliances form and how do they affect the conflict behavior of member countries? *See* Zeev Maoz, "Alliances: The Street Gangs of World Politics—Their Origins, Management, and Consequences, 1816–1986," in John A. Vasquez, ed., *What Do We Know About War?* (Lanham, MD: Rowman & Littlefield, 2000), pp. 111–144.

How does a sense of threat contribute to alliance formation and behavior? *See* Stephen M. Walt, *The Origins of Alliances* (Ithaca, NY: Cornell University Press, 1987).

Country Objectives

Minerite

Minerite is promoting the NPTO. Based in their capital city of Mamalode, the NPTO will include, among other clauses, a collective security arrangement for all members, a series of multilateral trade agreements that will facilitate economic development, and a cultural exchange program that is designed to cultivate artistic, social, and scientific collaboration among members. Because Minerite has close ties to its neighbor Paxony, and because Paxony remains one of the most powerful actors in Politica, it is imperative that Minerite convince Paxony to join the NPTO. Other countries such as Tundristan, Refugia, and Islandia would also give the NPTO the kind of legitimacy that Minerite is seeking. Because the NPTO is designed as a protective alliance against what Minerite perceives to be aggressive southern countries, however, Emerjant, Industrael, and Petropol should be excluded from the treaty. In order to achieve 10 objective points, Minerite must convince three other states to join the NPTO. This group of three states must include Paxony but exclude the southern trio of Emerjant, Industrael, and Petropol.

Emerjant

Emerjant does not believe that it is a good idea to polarize Politica into two competing alliance blocs, but the threatening nature of the NPTO necessitates that a counterbalancing coalition be formed. Because its southern neighbors have not shown any initiative of their own, Emerjant has decided that it must take a leadership position in creating the New Politican Bloc (NPB). The NPB is based in New Klowt. In addition to the obligatory mutual defense pact, the NPB also aims to increase the economic prosperity of the southern states. Emerjant leaders are most interested in having Industrael and Petropol as founding members of the NPB, but they feel that adding one or two northern countries would only strengthen the alliance. In addition, it would signal to the rest of Politica that, unlike Minerite, Emerjant does not aim to politically divide the system along north-south lines. In order to achieve 10 objective points, Emerjant must convince two countries to join the NPB. One of those countries must be Industrael, while any country (save for Minerite) could serve as the third member of the alliance.

Islandia

With a long history of neutrality and an interest in maintaining healthy commercial relations with all countries in Politica, Islandia is extremely reluctant to join either of the emerging alliances. In the past, Islandia has always played the role of "offshore balancer," and diplomatic flexibility is a fundamental aspect of Islandish foreign policy doctrine. Despite its close ties with Minerite, membership in the NPTO would likely send the wrong signal to the southern states that Islandia relies on for its export markets and natural resource access. Likewise, joining the NPB with Emerjant seems like a bad idea; longtime friends like Refugia and Paxony might think twice before doing business with Islandia in the future. Moreover, the large Ostracite population in Islandia would be in an uproar if the country joined an NPB that included Petropol. In order to achieve 5 objective points, Islandia must not join the NPTO or the NPB. In other words, Islandia must remain nonaligned in order to fulfill this objective.

Industrael

The once dominant Industrael is still strong enough to stand on its own. It certainly does not need to join any alliance in order to protect itself. Industrael's nuclear arsenal alone is sufficient to provide security. Still, after its recent defeat at the hand of Paxony, Industrael is somewhat wary of any sort of alliance that takes shape in the north. The idea of an NPTO that includes Minerite, Paxony, and other states is enough to trigger alarm in the Industraelite capital of Falmarx. Given such a development, the Industraelites would not be averse to a defense pact with their neighbors. That said, Industrael has no interest in a simple bilateral pact with Emerjant. That would simply make the once mighty Industrael a junior partner in a relatively weak alliance. If Industrael joins the NPB with

Emerjant, Petropol must be included in order to make the effort worthwhile. And the addition of one or more states such as Refugia or Tundristan would make the NPB even more attractive. In order to achieve 5 objective points, Industrael must either join the NPB if it includes both Emerjant and Petropol, or remain non-aligned if the NPB does not include both Emerjant and Petropol.

Refugia

With a long tradition of self-reliance, Refugia feels absolutely no need to join either of the proposed alliance organizations. Refugia's tendency toward isolation is also a result of the mistrust it has for Politican politics in general. Throughout history, the large Ostracite population in Refugia has been repeatedly attacked, persecuted, and betrayed by other countries. As a matter of survival, the Ostracites have adopted the philosophy of self-help. While they are happy to interact with other states when it comes to economic matters, they are firm believers in political and military nonalignment. In order to achieve 3 objective points, Refugia must stay true to this philosophy of nonalignment and refrain from signing either the NPTO or the NPB.

Petropol

For a number of reasons, Petropol has no incentive to join any alliance organization. First of all, Petropoleans have very few political friends in Politica. The northern countries of Minerite and Paxony might be useful as export markets, but military cooperation or political collaboration seems out of the question. In short, the NPTO has almost nothing to offer Petropol. While the NPB might be slightly more attractive (both Emerjant and Industrael are friendly states), joining a southern alliance might strain relations with the aforementioned northern states and thus reduce Petropolean oil revenues. And one thing is for sure, Petropol absolutely refuses to join any alliance that includes countries with a large Ostracite population such as Refugia or Islandia. In order to achieve 3 objective points, Petropol must refuse to sign on to either the NPTO or the NPB.

Paxony

Paxony is somewhat alarmed by the emerging divisions in Politica. After a long history of political confrontation and armed conflict, Paxons have grown tired of the competitive world of international politics. Still, Paxony has strong ties with Minerite and is very interested in the economic and cultural aspects of the NPTO. In order to achieve 1 objective point, Paxony must sign the NPTO.

Tundristan

In light of all its domestic turmoil, Tundristan is a country just looking for a little legitimacy. It has good relations with its neighbor Minerite, so joining the NPTO is appealing. Tundristan also has a healthy relationship with Petropol, so if that country joined the NPB, Tundristan would consider joining that organization as well. In order to achieve 1 objective point, Tundristan needs to join either the NPTO or the NPB, if the latter includes Petropol as a member.

Scenario Outcome Assessment
*Use this space to answer the question your instructor
has provided for this scenario*

Diplomatic Notes

Country Action Report

■ **Relevant Countries** (list all that are involved in action):

1.   5.

2.   6.

3.   7.

4.   8.

■ **Nature of Action** (what are these countries agreeing to do?):

■ **Required Signatures** (majority, including CDM, for democracies; CDM only for others):

	CDM	DIP	ECA	INT	OPP
Paxony					
Refugia					
Emerjant					
Tundristan					
Industrael					
Islandia					
Petropol					
Minerite					

8

Territorial Disputes

It is certainly no secret that Paxony and Industrael are staunch rivals. Countless wars (the last of which was particularly devastating) have forged a kind of social, cultural, and political animosity that is unmatched in Politica. Today, the focal point of this rivalry is the contested region of Centralia. The Kohridor River winds its way from west to east across the vast interior of Politica. At one point, the Kohridor splits into two large branches that connect once more hundreds of miles downstream. The land in between these two branches of the Kohridor is known as Centralia, for the native weed that grows along the banks of the river. Currently, Centralia is recognized as part of Paxony. After the last Great Paxon-Industraelite War, Paxony demanded the land as a spoil of victory. Because much of the Paxon countryside was devastated during the war, they felt entitled to additional, unspoiled lands such as Centralia. In the years since the war, Centralia has proven an invaluable source of agricultural and industrial wealth for Paxony. Socially, however, the postwar era has been defined by growing instability. Natives to the region identify much more with Industrael than with Paxony. The Industraelite government in Falmarx showered the Centralian people with special treatment in years past, but the Paxons seem more inclined to ignore the social and economic needs of the region. Thus, despite the general political liberalization that accompanied Paxon ownership, the local population has repeatedly called for reincorporation into Industrael. Small demonstrations and protests are growing larger and can no longer be ignored by the Paxon leadership in Berg. Recent reports from Centralia have hinted that local police and military units are resorting to violence as a means of suppression. With hundreds of thousands of people camped in city squares throughout Centralia, the situation is coming to a head. Will Paxony relent and give back this immensely valuable piece of land to Industrael? To what lengths will Industrael go in order to pressure Paxony on this matter? If Paxony returned Centralia

---

For Further Review: Territorial Disputes

Why do India and Pakistan care so much about the disputed Kashmir territory? *See* Sumantra Rose, *Kashmir: Roots of Conflict, Paths to Peace* (Cambridge, MA: Harvard University Press, 2003).

How often do territorial disputes lead to war? *See* Paul R. Hensel, "Charting a Course to Conflict: Territorial Issues and Interstate Conflict, 1816–1992," *Conflict Management and Peace Science* 15, no. 1 (1996): 43–74.

Why are neighboring countries more likely to fight? *See* John A. Vasquez, "Why Do Neighbors Fight? Proximity, Interaction, or Territoriality? *Journal of Peace Research* 32, no. 3 (1995): 277–293.

---

to Industrael, what kind of precedent would be set for similar cases in other parts of Politica?

| Country Objectives

Paxony

Paxony is stuck between a rock and a hard place in this scenario. Because the country is politically and socially liberal, it has a tradition of listening to its people. Its history as a multiethnic society has also created a general atmosphere of tolerance in Paxony. On the surface, then, it would seem as though Paxony would respond to the growing protests in Centralia by returning the region to Industrael. Above all else, this would make sense if Paxony truly were interested in reducing tensions with its historical rival. But, as usual, the situation is not that simple. Much of Paxony is still under reconstruction from the last war, and the country has relied heavily on Centralia, which was relatively untouched by fighting. Giving up the region would be devastating to the agricultural and industrial health of Paxony. Perhaps most worrisome is the precedent that returning this land would set. Paxony is a multiethnic state. There are a number of significant parts of the country that have local populations with strong ties to other states. In the north there is a large Minerite population in the Telon Highlands. In the southwest near the headwaters of the Kohridor River, the population is more likely to speak Emerjant than Paxon. In short, allowing Centralia to leave the Paxon state might create a domino effect that would encourage other groups to push for secession. The result could literally be the disintegration of Paxony. For 10 objective points, maintain possession of Centralia at all costs.

Industrael

Paxony has humiliated Industrael time and time again. By ignoring popular and diplomatic pressure to return Centralia to its rightful owner, Paxony would bring Industraelite prestige to an all-time low. Already a country in economic and political decline, Industrael cannot afford to be pushed around anymore. In the capital city of Falmarx, the highest priority is securing the return of Centralia to Industrael. The government has staked its reputation on success on this issue, and it is willing to go to great lengths in order to get Paxony to relent. The authoritarian regime in Industrael is certainly not known for its compassion, but there is an undeniably humanitarian aspect of this crisis. How can a country like Paxony, that prides itself on being a liberal democracy, ignore the pleas of such a large population? Perhaps it is time for Industrael to step back into the global spotlight by successfully revealing the hypocritical stance taken by Paxony. Not only would there be reputational benefits to staring down Paxony, reincorporating Centralia might be just the economic jumpstart that the ailing Industraelite economy needs. For 10 objective points, use whatever means necessary to regain full control over Centralia.

Minerite

The Minerite leadership is torn on this issue. It has had a long running dispute with Paxony over the Minerite population living in the northern region of that country. More than once, the otherwise airtight friendship between the two countries has been cracked by conflict over Minerite's desire to expand its boundaries to include these populations. Paxony has never budged an inch on the issue, so it is not surprising that they are highly resistant to the idea of returning an important region like Centralia to Industrael. Certain radical factions in the capital of Mamalode have suggested that Minerite should pressure Paxony to cave on the Centralia issue; perhaps such an action would set an important precedent that would eventually lead to the reunification of the Paxony Minerites with their historical homeland. More conservative politicians in Minerite, however, point out that picking a fight with Paxony right now is ill advised. Paxony is a sought-after alliance partner and counterbalance to the growing powers in the south. The reunification issue is simply not worth pressing. In order to achieve 5 objective points, Minerite must support Paxony in its efforts to retain control of Centralia. If Paxony fails in this effort, Minerite fails this objective.

Tundristan

Put simply, Tundristan is very interested in making sure that Centralia remains in Paxon hands. If the local population's protests were sufficient to cause a transfer in ownership, a dangerous precedent would be set. For several years, the semiautonomous Ostracite homeland in western Tundristan has been calling for complete independence. Economically, politically, and socially, this would spell disaster for Tundristan as a whole. Enormous, violent protests (larger than those in Centralia) have rocked the Tundrek capital and several other major cities. Tundristan has responded with strength and has used a wide range of strategies for suppressing the independence movement. Outside governments have accused Tundristan of systematic persecution and the killing of Ostracites. If Paxony were to cave on the Centralia issue, it would not be long before there was increased pressure on Tundristan to back down in similar fashion and grant independence to the Ostracites. For 5 objective points, make sure that Paxony resists pressure to return Centralia to Industrael.

Islandia

From a political standpoint, Islandia is inclined to support Paxony on this issue. This may even be the case if economic interests are paramount. But in some cases, moral concerns trump all others. Islandia really has no direct interest in Centralia, although it would like to see the notion of self-determination applied as often as possible. This is particularly the case when it comes to the Ostracite population in Tundristan. Islandia has a large Ostracite population itself, and has long sought protection for them around the world. In light of the alleged persecution of Ostracites in Tundristan, full independence for the Ostracite homeland seems well justified. If Centralia is returned to Industrael due to popular pressure, perhaps the same outcome will be more likely in Tundristan. For 3 objective points, pressure Paxony to return Centralia to Industrael. If the land is not returned, Islandia fails this objective.

Emerjant

Like many other states in Politica, Emerjant has very little at stake in Centralia itself. But the outcome there may have important consequences for an isolated group of ethnic Emerjants in southern Paxony. This group is based in the southern foothills of the Longa Mountain chain, near the headwaters of the Kohridor River. Emerjant has consistently claimed this land as their own, and the local population speaks Emerjant and adheres to Emerjant customs. Because of the strategic importance of this region, Paxony has repeatedly refused to allow its incorporation into Emerjant. In light of their designs for the "Grand Kohridor Dam Project," it is unlikely that Paxony will relent in the future. Still, if a precedent can be set in Centralia, the potential for change will be increased. For 3 objective points, join Industrael and pressure Paxony to return control of Centralia.

Petropol

The imperial powers of Politica always seem to be squabbling. What happens in Centralia is of no real importance to the Petropoleans. The only concern is that Industrael will turn its attention to the east if its territorial ambitions are stymied in the west. This might lead Industrael to entertain thoughts of expansion at Petropol's expense. Keep Industrael satisfied in the west by helping it reacquire Centralia. Petropol will score 1 objective point if the land is returned.

Refugia

Like Petropol, Refugia has no interest in the Centralia issue. In fact, its only concern is the prevention of armed conflict. Its large Ostracite population always ends up suffering as scapegoats when the dogs of war are unleashed. Regardless of the political outcome, Refugia will achieve 1 objective point if the situation in Centralia does not lead to a declaration of war.

Scenario Outcome Assessment

*Use this space to answer the question your instructor
has provided for this scenario*

Diplomatic Notes

Country Action Report

■ Relevant Countries (list all that are involved in action):

1.   5.

2.   6.

3.   7.

4.   8.

■ Nature of Action (what are these countries agreeing to do?):

■ Required Signatures (majority, including CDM, for democracies; CDM only for others):

	CDM	DIP	ECA	INT	OPP
Paxony					
Refugia					
Emerjant					
Tundristan					
Industrael					
Islandia					
Petropol					
Minerite					

9 | Nuclear Proliferation

The Petropolean theocracy has adamantly protected its citizens from the spoiling influence of modern culture. And while a certain sector of the country has prospered under this traditional approach, the general isolation of Petropolean society has prevented the country as a whole from emerging as an important player in Politican politics. Oil revenue goes mostly to the privileged elite class and is rarely invested in a way that promotes long-term growth. As a result, Petropol is very rarely taken seriously at any international bargaining table. For years, this was not a problem for Petropolean leaders. But as oil wealth has grown in the country, so has the desire for political prestige and respect. In the minds of the political, petroleum, and religious elite, the quickest way to achieve this respect is by acquiring a sizeable nuclear arsenal.

Oil wealth and a cadre of highly educated scientists make this a viable option for Petropol. In fact, a parade was recently held in the city of Norau to celebrate groundbreaking on a state-of-the-art nuclear facility. Petropolean leaders have maintained that any weapons will be reserved for defensive purposes only, but this statement has been met by uniform incredulity across capital cities in Politica. Particularly concerned are the existing nuclear powers of Paxony and Industrael. These two countries have established a transparent arms control regime that has greatly reduced the possibility of nuclear war. In just the past year, an agreement was reached that would entirely eliminate nuclear weapons in Politica within ten years. A Petropolean bomb would not only reverse this trend of disarmament, it would likely lead to a new arms race between Paxony and Industrael. Protests have been particularly frequent and loud from Refugia. It is no secret that the Petropoleans and ethnic Ostracites in Refugia harbor an intense dislike for each other. In years past, radical Petropolean leaders have boasted that—given the chance—they would push Refugia back into the Placidic Sea. Refugia has made it clear that a Petropolean bomb would be followed closely by

---

For Further Review: Nuclear Proliferation

Could nuclear proliferation actually increase international stability? *See* Kenneth N. Waltz, "More May Be Better," in Scott D. Sagan and Kenneth N. Waltz, *The Spread of Nuclear Weapons: A Debate Renewed* (New York: W.W. Norton, 2003).

Does Iran want a nuclear arsenal? *See* Shahram Chubin and Rob Litwak, "Debating Iran's Nuclear Aspirations," *Washington Quarterly* 26, no. 4 (2003): 99–114.

Will nuclear proliferation lead to nuclear terrorism? *See* Graham T. Allison, *Nuclear Terrorism: The Ultimate Preventable Catastrophe* (New York: Times Books, 2004).

---

a Refugee bomb. Should Petropol be allowed to develop its own nuclear arsenal? If so, do other countries deserve the same option? To what lengths are certain countries willing to go in order to prevent proliferation?

Country Objectives

Petropol

According to Petropolean leaders in Norau, a nuclear arsenal is the right of each and every sovereign state in Politica. They have repeatedly accused the rest of the world of hypocrisy when it comes to the issue of nuclear proliferation. Petropol feels that Paxony and Industrael have held the world hostage with their nuclear weapons for decades. Its leaders point out that, while Paxony claims a Petropolean bomb would be a threat to international security, Paxony is the only country to have used a nuclear weapon in battle.

Beyond its philosophical justification for pursuing nuclear weapons, Petropol is also interested in the political prestige and leverage that possession of such weapons will generate. For many years, Petropol has been disregarded as an important player in Politican politics. This was not of much importance while oil revenues streamed in from the rest of the world, but recent international competition in the oil industry has made political leverage an important prerequisite for economic prosperity. In short, the primary purpose of acquiring nuclear weapons is to increase leverage at the bargaining table. A healthy oil industry is absolutely vital to the Petropolean government. Because much of its population tolerates the politically repressive government because of the wealth it provides them, a drop in living standards could be a recipe for revolution. If Petropol withstands international pressure and follows through with its nuclear ambitions, it will earn 10 objective points. If Petropol abandons its goal of possessing nuclear weapons in any way, it fails this objective.

Refugia

A nuclear weapon in the hands of the Petropolean government would be an unmitigated disaster for the Refugees. While Refugia does not relish the fact that Paxony and Industrael have nuclear arsenals capable of destroying Politica a dozen times over, a Petropolean bomb is much more troubling because of that country's stated intention of—in the words of a previous Petropolean leader—"incinerating" Refugia and its Ostracite population. Refugia could respond to a nuclear attack; it is widely accepted that the country has secretly developed its own nuclear arsenal over the years. It has never acknowledged that such an arsenal exists, but there is evidence of extensive uranium enrichment and even underground tests conducted in the western reaches of the Longa Mountains. Because of its small size, however, even one nuclear explosion would inflict unacceptable damage on Refugia. If Petropol develops a nuclear arsenal, leaders in Sansafe are convinced that the only way to deter it from attacking is for Refugia to disclose its own nuclear capability and threaten a massive counterstrike in response to any attack. Thus the first priority for Refugia is to work (alone or with allies) to prevent Petropol from following through on its stated intention to develop nuclear weapons. If Refugia is successful, it will achieve 10 objective points. But in the event that Petropol does go nuclear, Refugia can also earn 10 points if it publicly announces its own nuclear capability.

Paxony

Paxony is the only country to have used nuclear weapons in conflict. After seven years of fighting during the last Paxon-Industraelite War, advancing Industraelite forces were on the brink of capturing the Paxon capital of Berg. In what they perceived as a desperate situation, Paxony's leadership decided to use their very first—newly developed and untested—nuclear bomb as a last-ditch effort to avoid defeat.

The results of the attack were staggering. Militarily, the bomb changed the entire complexion of the war and ultimately led to Paxony's victory. The environmental and social consequences of the blast are still being felt today. The blast zone—inside Paxon territory—is still uninhabitable. The human toll is being realized in terms of physical and psychological destruction. As a result of its intimate experience with nuclear weapons, Paxony has been a vocal proponent of disarmament in Politica. While political confrontation with Industrael has made this difficult, Paxony has taken big steps in reducing its own arsenal and working with Industrael to stabilize a volatile situation. If Petropol were to follow through on its stated intention to develop nuclear weapons, nonproliferation efforts would suffer a huge setback. This would also be the case if Refugia were to publicly declare its nuclear capability. If Paxony can keep Petropol from developing and Refugia from declaring their nuclear capability, it will earn 5 objective points.

Emerjant

Emerjant is not a nuclear country, and it finds the thought of a Refugee or Petropolean bomb particularly unsettling. If such a situation were to develop, Emerjant would find itself completely surrounded by members of the nuclear club: Refugia, Paxony, Industrael, and Petropol. Unlike Petropol and Refugia, Emerjant does not have the technical sophistication or uranium stockpiles necessary to develop a nuclear deterrent of its own. In many other ways, Emerjant is very much in favor of overturning the status quo in Politica. In this situation, however, the stakes are just too high. Emerjant will achieve this 5 point objective if neither Petropol nor Refugia become nuclear powers.

Industrael

Shortly after its forces were devastated by Paxony's nuclear attack, Industrael committed itself to developing a nuclear arsenal of its own. It was successful in doing so, and the ensuing decades have been characterized by rough nuclear parity between the two powers. Industrael has cooperated with Paxony when it comes to arms reduction, but a large portion of Industraelite society has mourned the loss of weapons that have granted them so much legitimacy over the years. As Industrael's economy continues to sag and its leverage vis-à-vis Paxony declines, some have called for revamping Industrael's nuclear proficiency. As part of this effort, a number of Industraelite scientists have visited neighboring Petropol in order to learn about the very latest in nuclear weapons technology. The Petropoleans have pledged to share their superior technology and know-how with Industrael in exchange for Industrael's political support of the Petropolean nuclear program. After much deliberation, Industraelite leaders have decided to accept this offer. Industrael will earn 3 objective points if Petropol is able to follow through and establish its nuclear weapons capability.

Tundristan

Like Industrael, Tundristan supports the Petropolean nuclear program. It has a very close relationship with Petropol and there is some hope that Petropol might be willing to aid Tundristan if it were to pursue nuclear weapons capability in the future. If proliferation were to become the norm in Politica, Tundristan might be able to go nuclear without the political uproar that the current scenario has generated. There is no doubt that a nuclear deterrent would be quite valuable in resisting international pressure to recognize the Ostracite homeland as fully independent. It might even be appropriate for dealing with the Ostracites themselves. Tundristan will achieve 3 objective points if Petropol is able to follow through and establish its nuclear weapons capability.

Islandia

At one point, Islandia had the ability to acquire its own nuclear deterrent. It declined that opportunity and since that time has had no interest whatsoever in nuclear weapons or the politics that go along with them. As a commercially based society, the Islandish are most fearful of war and the economic disruption it would cause. Thus, Islandia can earn 1 objective point simply by ensuring that the current crisis does not involve any declarations of war.

Minerite

Like Islandia, Minerite wants no part of the complex world of nuclear politics. While a Petropolean bomb (or a Refugee bomb for that matter) is not a comforting thought, Minerite is not concerned about being the target of a nuclear attack. Still, it experienced enormous damage as the result of fallout from the Paxon nuclear attack on Industraelite forces. This has created a determined antinuclear lobby in Minerite. In order to satisfy this lobby, Minerite is compelled to oppose a Petropolean or Refugee bomb. If neither country goes nuclear, Minerite will meet this 1 point objective.

Scenario Outcome Assessment

*Use this space to answer the question your instructor
has provided for this scenario*

Diplomatic Notes

Country Action Report

■ **Relevant Countries** (list all that are involved in action):

1.   5.

2.   6.

3.   7.

4.   8.

■ **Nature of Action** (what are these countries agreeing to do?):

■ **Required Signatures** (majority, including CDM, for democracies; CDM only for others):

	CDM	DIP	ECA	INT	OPP
Paxony					
Refugia					
Emerjant					
Tundristan					
Industrael					
Islandia					
Petropol					
Minerite					

10
Ethnic Conflict

The news out of Tundristan is alarming. For a number of years, residents of the semiautonomous Ostracite homeland in western Tundristan have longed for full independence. Although the oft-persecuted Ostracites were grateful for the invitation to establish permanent and protected settlements in Tundristan, they accepted the offer with an understanding that those permanent settlements would one day be allowed to achieve sovereign status in Politica. To date, the Tundrek government in Wasibad has stymied efforts at independence. With the recent discovery of significant oil deposits in the region, the possibility of an independent Ostracite state in Tundristan seems remote. This development in itself is not terribly troubling, but recent events suggest that a tragedy could be in the making.

A number of independent observers has reported that the Tundrek government has resorted to widespread and systematic violence in response to proindependence demonstrations in the Ostracite homeland. Arrested protesters are being held indefinitely and prevented from communicating with friends or relatives. There are rumors that the government has even extended its crackdown to include Ostracites in rural areas that have had nothing to do with the largely urban-based independence movement. Evidence of political assassinations, kidnapping, and public execution is beginning to mount. Some are going so far as to call the events characteristic of genocide. For their part, the Ostracites are thought to be responsible for a recent spate of deadly suicide bomb attacks in the eastern, non-Ostracite regions of Tundristan. The international community is at an impasse: What exactly is going on in Tundristan? Can Tundristan be persuaded to end the confrontation by allowing for an independent Ostracite homeland? Are reports of genocide exaggerated, or is the world on the brink of allowing another tragedy to befall the Ostracites? Will the powers that be in Wasibad acquiesce and allow an international investigation of alleged human rights abuses?

For Further Review: Ethnic Conflict

When is it right to intervene? *See* J. L. Holzgrefe and Robert O. Keohane, eds., *Humanitarian Intervention: Ethical, Legal and Political Dilemmas* (Cambridge, UK: Cambridge University Press, 2003).

What is the history of ethnic conflict in international relations? *See* Ted R. Gurr and Barbara Harff, *Ethnic Conflict in World Politics* (Boulder, CO: Westview, 1994).

What actually happened, and what will happen in Darfur? *See* Scott Straus, "Darfur and the Genocide Debate," *Foreign Affairs* 84, no. 1 (2005): 123–133.

Country Objectives

Tundristan

Ethnic-based conflict is always a sensitive issue, particularly when the Ostracites are involved. But the Tundreks maintain that clashes with proindependence demonstrators are in no way part of a larger effort to persecute the broader Ostracite population. If anything, it is the Ostracites who should be condemned for the unprovoked suicide bombings they have used to attack innocent Tundrek civilians. Any forceful action in the Ostracite homeland is simply a response to the provocations of the increasingly aggressive independence movement in the region. Tundristan vehemently denies any accusations of human rights abuse. Key officials assert that reports of political assassination, kidnapping, or detainment are simply the result of the Ostracite propaganda machine. Despite repeated requests from the human welfare division of the PSF, Tundristan has steadfastly refused to permit an international investigation. Why should a sovereign state like Tundristan be forced to submit to a humiliating investigation when it has done nothing wrong?

Although it is tempting for Tundristan to back down to meet Ostracite demands for full independence, the economic consequences would be disastrous; the vast majority of Tundristan's oil wealth is found in the Ostracite homeland. Even in the absence of such economic imperatives, there is absolutely no precedent in Politican politics that would suggest that a group can justify secession simply because they prefer greater autonomy. Tundristan is not prepared to set this precedent by being the first to offer independence to all who ask. To achieve this 10 point objective, Tundristan must resist any and all calls for an international investigation into alleged human rights abuses. In addition, Tundristan must prevent the Ostracite homeland from achieving political independence.

Islandia

Islandia is gravely concerned about the situation in Tundristan. While there is no proof that the Tundreks are engaging in systematic violence against the Ostracites, it is always better to err on the side of caution when there is a potential genocide taking place. The large population of Ostracites in Islandia makes the crisis in Tundristan even more alarming for most Islandish. Islandia has long suspected Tundristan of persecuting its Ostracite population, and has been a leading proponent of the establishment of an independent state in Tundristan for the Ostracites. With new evidence of violent repression pouring in every day, Islandia is willing to go to great lengths in order to establish such a state. Along with Refugia, Islandish leaders have offered to increase already large amounts of foreign aid to Tundristan in return for recognition of Ostracite sovereignty. In addition, Islandia has used its permanent seat on the PSF to coordinate an international investigation into the alleged human rights abuses by Tundristan. Thus far, however, the PSF has not been allowed into Tundristan. International media and political organizations have only been let into the country to briefly photograph the gruesome aftermath of suicide bombings in Wasibad. The Tundreks allege that the Ostracites are responsible for these attacks. Being proactive in this scenario is crucial to Islandia; in order to achieve this 10 point objective, Islandia must convince Tundristan to allow a full investigation by the PSF into alleged human rights violations against the Ostracites. More importantly, the Islandish must also get the Tundreks to recognize the Ostracite homeland as a fully independent, sovereign state.

Refugia

No state has closer ties to the Ostracites in Tundristan than Refugia. Decades ago, Refugia was an important partner in the Ostracites's search for a homeland along the coast of the Placidic Sea. With such a close connection to Ostracites in Tundristan, the Refugees have a strong sense of duty to protect that population. Along with Islandia, Refugia has been quick to publicize any reports of alleged human rights violations against the Ostracites. A Refugee spokesperson in Sansafe went so far as to suggest that the Tundreks have staged the suicide bombings in Wasibad in order to portray the Ostracite proindependence movement as more violent than it really is.

Although it does not have a permanent seat on the PSF, Refugia has worked with Islandia (which does have a permanent seat) in order to secure the right to investigate the situation in the Ostracite homeland firsthand. Industrael and Paxony—the other two permanent members—have been reluctant to act against Tundristan because of political considerations. While Refugia is not determined to secure independence for the Ostracite homeland, it will not settle for anything less than a full-scale investigation by the PSF. If Refugia convinces (or compels) Tundristan to accept such an investigation, it will achieve this 5 point objective.

Petropol

Petropol would be shocked if its close friends the Tundreks were guilty of anything more than self-defense in their confrontation with the Ostracites. It is the Ostracites that should be suspected of foul play. Are they not the instigators of violence, with their massive protests and cowardly suicide bombings? The Ostracites have a long tradition of exaggerating any political opposition they face. The Tundreks were gracious in allowing them a semiautonomous homeland. There is no moral or legal justification for an independent Ostracite state to be carved out of territory that rightfully belongs to Tundristan. Likewise, a forced investigation by the PSF would be a gross violation of Tundrek sovereignty. Petropol vehemently opposes any such investigation and would abhor the creation of an independent Ostracite state in Tundrek territory. If it is able to prevent either event from occurring, Petropol will score 5 objective points.

Paxony

On the surface, it would seem as though Paxony would lead the charge when it comes to investigating potential human rights abuses. The Paxons take a great deal of pride when it comes to ethical matters in Politica—it has often used its permanent seat on the PSF to press for democratization in places like Tundristan and Emerjant. Recently, Paxony has even proposed the creation of the Politican Court of Justice (PCJ) in Berg. Predictably, Paxony would be happy to lead an PSF investigation into potential human rights abuses in Tundristan. But Paxon leaders have been strangely silent when it comes to Ostracite independence. Off the record, high-ranking officials have acknowledged that Paxony is worried about the creation of an independent Ostracite state in Tundristan. Such a development would stretch the concept of self-determination beyond what is beneficial to a multiethnic society like Paxony. From Centralia in the south to the Telon Highlands in the north, Paxony is intent on maintaining control over several regional populations that have begun to clamor for independence. Given domestic considerations, Paxony is simultaneously in favor of an international human rights investigation but opposed to the formation of an independent Ostracite state in Tundristan. It will fail this 3 point objective if an investigation is not allowed in Tundristan. But it will also fail if independence is granted to the Ostracites.

Minerite

Minerite has very practical considerations in mind when it comes to the unrest in Tundristan. Like much of Politica, the Minerites are in favor of an international investigation into alleged human rights abuses in Tundristan. But the political costs that would accompany an independent Ostracite homeland are too excessive to garner Minerite support. With Tundristan's resource-rich western region taken from it, the country would likely attempt to expand eastward across the Pella Canal and into Minerite. At the very least, this would result in diplomatic tension between Minerite and Tundristan at a time when maintaining Tundristan's friendship is high on the Minerite agenda. In order to meet this 3 point objective, Minerite must prevent the creation of an independent Ostracite homeland in what is today western Tundristan.

Industrael

With no close ties to the Ostracites and a history of political repression at home, it is not surprising that Industrael opposes both an independent state in the Ostracite homeland as well as a PSF-led investigation into alleged human rights abuses against the Ostracites. If necessary, Industrael will use the veto power that comes along with its permanent seat on the PSF in order to prevent such an investigation from occurring. If it is successful in preventing an investigation and thwarting Ostracite independence, Industrael will earn 1 objective point.

Emerjant

As a founding member of the New Politican Bloc, Emerjant is encouraging Tundristan to join the alliance. Tundristan has been reluctant, but perhaps Emerjant can foster a sense of friendship with Tundristan by opposing both the creation of an independent state in the Ostracite homeland and any international investigation into potential human rights abuses. If this opposition is successful, Emerjant will earn 1 objective point.

Scenario Outcome Assessment

*Use this space to answer the question your instructor
has provided for this scenario*

Diplomatic Notes

Country Action Report

■ **Relevant Countries** (list all that are involved in action):

1.   5.

2.   6.

3.   7.

4.   8.

■ **Nature of Action** (what are these countries agreeing to do?):

■ **Required Signatures** (majority, including CDM, for democracies; CDM only for others):

	CDM	DIP	ECA	INT	OPP
Paxony					
Refugia					
Emerjant					
Tundristan					
Industrael					
Islandia					
Petropol					
Minerite					

11

Free Trade vs. Protectionism

Advances in transportation and communication technology have made it easier for Politican states to trade with each other. Although societies have bartered and exchanged goods for centuries, the modern era has seen an explosion in international trade. Sea lanes and highways are filled with goods being sent from one part of Politica to another. At the same time sardines from Tundristan are being shipped to the Petropolean desert, computers from Islandia are landing at Emerjant harbors in the South Placidic Sea. Through the principles of absolute and comparative advantage, it is easy to see that—as a whole—Politica is able to increase its total economic output via strategies of specialization and trade. In this day and age there is no country in Politica that produces absolutely everything its society needs within its own borders. On the surface, it appears as though all countries benefit from the concept of a global marketplace where goods are totally free to change hands at prices set by the laws of supply and demand.

In an effort to formalize the idea of a free and open global marketplace, Minerite and Islandia are proposing a Politican Trade Organization (PTO). Members of the PTO would agree to eliminate the remaining obstacles to international trade. Tariff and nontariff barriers would be abolished; import quotas would be forbidden. Proponents of the PTO argue that only via such a strategy can the true economic potential of the Politican people be realized. Once the policies of the PTO are put in place, imports will be cheaper and foreign export markets will grow. Each country will be able to specialize in its most efficient areas and trade for goods it needs from elsewhere. But some countries are reluctant to join the PTO. Are the concepts of free trade and open markets really beneficial for all those involved? Does reliance on foreign imports carry a price tag of vulnerability? Leaders in Petropol, Tundristan, and Industrael point out that the PTO may just be another money-making plot by the rich countries in Politica.

> ### For Further Review: Free Trade vs. Protectionism
>
> Is globalization and free trade good for everyone? *See* Ethan B. Kapstein, "Winners and Losers in the Global Economy," *International Organization* 54 (2000): 359–384.
>
> How has the concept of free trade evolved over the years? *See* Lars Magnusson, *The Tradition of Free Trade* (New York: Routledge, 2004).
>
> What is the global impact of the World Trade Organization? *See* Bernard Hoekman and Michael Kostecki, *The Political Economy of the World Trading System: WTO and Beyond* (Oxford: Oxford University Press, 2001).

Country Objectives

Minerite

Minerite has big plans for itself. In the next twenty years, it would like to be mentioned in the same breath as great powers like Paxony, Industrael, and Islandia. To achieve heightened status in Politica, the Minerite economy must continue to grow. Recent expansion has been nothing to sneeze at, but in order to maintain its current economic expansion, Minerite corporations must have free access to foreign markets. Presently, Minerite has bilateral free trade agreements with commercially minded countries such as Paxony and Islandia. But other states, such as Industrael, Tundristan, and Petropol have stubbornly maintained various forms of economic protectionism. For example: Although Minerite can deliver mineral resources to Tundrek industry cheaper than mining companies in Tundristan itself, a quota on Minerite imports limits access to the Tundrek market. Likewise, a preferential agreement between Petropol and Industrael means that Minerite oil is heavily restricted in the Industraelite market.

For Minerite, the PTO is a solution to the economic protectionism that restricts economic growth. All the Minerites are asking for is a level playing field. Countries that join the PTO would simply agree to play by the rules of the free market. Given a fighting chance, Minerite is convinced that its economy will propel it to great power status in the very near future. If Minerite can get six additional countries to join the PTO, it will achieve this 10 point objective.

Industrael

Countries that constantly favor the principles of free trade and open markets ignore the fact that economics is about more than efficiency and total output. Industrael is staunchly against the PTO because it will result in the destruction of several of its industrial sectors and the loss of millions of jobs to foreign competition. Industrael has a long history as an industrial powerhouse in Politica. During the height of its rivalry with Paxony, Industraelite textile mills and steel factories out-produced the rest of Politica combined. Today, these industries have fallen behind the times. On a per-unit basis, the cost of producing a ton of steel in Industrael is almost twice the global average. If Industrael were to sign the PTO and open its domestic market to foreign steel imports, the results would be disastrous. The same is true for a number of sectors in the Industraelite economy. The only way to keep factories open and jobs in place is to maintain tariff barriers and quotas on imports. This would be impossible if Industrael were to join the PTO. If it is able to resist international pressure to join the organization, and can also convince either Tundristan or Petropol to do the same, Industrael will score 10 objective points.

Refugia

Despite a small economy that is less than competitive in a number of ways, Refugia supports the PTO because it believes firmly in the long-term benefits of economic interdependence. Although its nascent industrial sector will likely suffer if exposed to competition from Islandia or Minerite, the Refugees will find large markets for their cherished fishing industry. Most importantly, a world that is intertwined economically is a world that is less likely to go to war. Economic interdependence, in the minds of the Refugees, is much more important in preventing conflict than is regime type or social similarity. For a country that is always vulnerable in times of war, a strong and healthy PTO might be the best security blanket available. Perhaps the best way to improve relations with Tundristan or Petropol is to engage them in trade. In order to score 5 objective points, Refugia needs to join the PTO and make sure that no fewer than five other countries join them.

Islandia

Islandish always have been and always will be commercially minded people. The idea of an organization that promotes free trade and open markets throughout Politica is unquestionably appealing. If the PTO is going to create a global marketplace in Politica, Islandia will be more than happy to sign on. Because the Islandish economy is the most technologically advanced in Politica, leaders in Harbur are confident about their country's ability to compete on a level playing field. If present restrictions on high-tech imports to Tundristan and Petropol are lifted, economists estimate that Islandia's economy will grow an additional 5 to 10 percent per year. If Islandia joins the PTO and is able to convince both Tundristan and Petropol to do the same, it will achieve this 5 point objective.

Emerjant

This country's economic miracle has been fueled by a healthy appetite for Emerjant exports. Emerjant has benefited immensely from the general absence of foreign tariffs on its goods. In order to maintain the growth it is accustomed to, Emerjant will need to make sure that additional markets are opened; while trade with rivals such as Tundristan is not likely to grow in the near future, erasing existing barriers to trade with allies such as Industrael and Petropol will be a great way to build economic prosperity at home while fostering political cooperation abroad. Given recent signs that Emerjant might be falling out of favor with some investors, an export boom would be even more valuable as a way to restore confidence in the country's long-term growth prospects. In order to achieve this 3 point objective, Emerjant must join the PTO and convince either Industrael or Petropol to do the same.

Tundristan

Is it really the case that all countries in Politica are better off when they specialize, engage in free trade, and open their markets to foreign competition? In Tundristan, there is a consensus that economic growth has been hampered by continued specialization in the production of commodities like iron and sardines. The price of these commodities is quite volatile and invariably quite low compared to the automobiles and televisions Tundreks must import from abroad. In short, Tundristan has decided that the global economic game is rigged. If it continues to play by the rules, Tundristan will never prosper. Regardless of what other countries think, Tundristan is against joining the PTO. If it refuses to do so, it will earn 3 objective points.

Paxony

Joining the PTO will not change much in Paxony—it already has free trade agreements with its most important economic partners. That said, the country would love to have greater access to the Tundristan market, and increased economic interaction with Industrael could lead to a thaw in the political relationship with that country. If Paxony joins the PTO and can convince either Tundristan or Industrael to do the same, it will earn 1 objective point.

Petropol

Petropol does not have to worry much about securing markets for its exports. Since it controls 40 percent of Politica's known oil reserves, foreign markets pretty much come begging on hands and knees. The PTO is more threatening than helpful; the Petropolean theocracy likes having the right to restrict what comes into the country. This would be impossible if it joined the PTO. If Petropol manages to stay out of that organization, it will earn 1 objective point.

Scenario Outcome Assessment

Use this space to answer the question your instructor
has provided for this scenario

Diplomatic Notes

Country Action Report

■ Relevant Countries (list all that are involved in action):

1.   5.

2.   6.

3.   7.

4.   8.

■ Nature of Action (what are these countries agreeing to do?):

■ Required Signatures (majority, including CDM, for democracies; CDM only for others):

	CDM	DIP	ECA	INT	OPP
Paxony					
Refugia					
Emerjant					
Tundristan					
Industrael					
Islandia					
Petropol					
Minerite					

12
Natural Resource Politics

From its headwaters in the Longa Mountains, the Kohridor River flows across the heart of Politica. Along the way, the waters of the Kohridor serve as the industrial and agricultural lifeblood of countries like Emerjant, Industrael, and Minerite. Other states such as Petropol attach great religious significance to the wide and powerful river. But no country relies more on the Kohridor River than Paxony; for well over a thousand miles, the river serves as its southern and eastern border. Along the way, its waters are used to power Paxon industry and irrigate Paxon farms; a full 40 percent of the Paxon population resides within 20 miles of the Kohridor.

At the last meeting of the PSF, Paxony unveiled plans for the Grand Kohridor Dam Project, a series of massive dams that will be used to produce hydroelectric power and divert water for use in the Paxon agricultural sector. Most of the dams will be constructed near the headwaters of the river in the Longa Mountains of western Paxony. The steep elevation drop and proximity to the majority of Paxon farms make this an ideal location. To say the least, this proposal has caused quite a stir in Politica. Leading opponents include Emerjant, Industrael, and Petropol. These countries point out that the Kohridor should be treated as a common resource for all countries in Politica. By asserting control of the headwaters of the Kohridor, Paxony has the ability to hold downriver countries hostage with the threat of reduced flow. Even more important, the pristine nature of the river will be forever spoiled by the presence of gigantic dams and extensive diversion canals. Can Paxony garner any support for the Grand Kohridor Dam Project? Given that all construction will take place within Paxon borders, do opponents of the project have any leverage to prevent its completion? Is there a way for Paxony to compensate affected countries in order to secure support?

For Further Review: Natural Resource Politics

Will environmental scarcity become an even greater source of conflict in the future? *See* Thomas Homer-Dixon, *Environment, Scarcity, and Violence* (Princeton, NJ: Princeton University Press, 1999).

How has the control of scarce water played a role in the history of violence in the Middle East? *See* John K. Cooley, "The War over Water," in Richard K. Betts, ed., *Conflict After the Cold War: Arguments on Causes of War and Peace* (New York: Pearson, 2005), pp. 557–566.

What are the consequences of Turkey's Southeastern Anatolia Project? *See* L. M. Harris, "Water and Conflict Geographies of the Southeastern Anatolia Project," *Society and Natural Resources* 15, no. 8 (2002): 743–760.

Country Objectives

Paxony

The Grand Kohridor Dam Project is the largest public works project ever attempted in Politica. After it is completed, it will produce enough hydroelectric power to satisfy 28 percent of Paxony's entire energy demand. Farmers in the heavily agricultural southern regions of Paxony will benefit from the construction of diversion canals that will take water directly from the Kohridor to their fields. Paxony has gone to great lengths in order to convince other states along the Kohridor that the project will not affect them in any significant way. Although water flow will be somewhat reduced because of the diversion canals, Paxon hydrologists have concluded that this reduction will have a negligible impact on downriver states. Conservative estimates suggest that the project will only result in a 1–2 percent reduction in industrial output for Emerjant, Industrael, Minerite, and Petropol. Leaders in Berg have hinted that they may be open to the idea of compensating certain states for the economic damage they might suffer as a result of the dams and diversion canals.

Paxony has invested quite a bit of political capital in securing international support for the Grand Kohridor Dam Project. While it wants to go ahead with construction regardless of international opinion (construction is taking place entirely within Paxon borders), Paxony might be forced to reconsider if Emerjant, Industrael, Minerite, and Petropol all speak out against the project. If Paxony can complete the Grand Kohridor Dam Project with support from at least two of the four countries mentioned above, it will achieve this 10 point objective.

Petropol

The Kohridor River is a source of spiritual inspiration for the Petropolean people. Furthermore, they firmly believe that the river is a resource to be shared among all of the countries it runs through. There is strong opposition in Petropol to the proposed Grand Kohridor Dam Project. The fact that the headwaters of the Kohridor happen to fall within Paxon borders does not give Paxony the right to destroy the purity of the Kohridor on a whim. Monetary compensation cannot buy Petropolean support for the dams and diversion canals; millions of Petropoleans visit the banks of the Kohridor each year as part of an ancient religious pilgrimage. If the waters of the Kohridor are spoiled by the greed of Paxony and other states, it will lose the spiritual essence that makes it a holy site for Petropoleans. In Petropol, the completion of the Grand Kohridor Dam Project would cause unprecedented social disruption. Using whatever means possible, Petropol must convince Paxony to abandon construction. If it is successful in doing so, Petropol will earn 10 objective points.

Emerjant

Although it has no religious or social objection to the Grand Kohridor Dam Project, Emerjant opposes the project on economic and political grounds. Economically, the industrial area along the south bank of the Kohridor River would be affected by the dams and diversion canals. Emerjant scientists and economists estimate that even a small reduction of water flow in the Kohridor could reduce industrial output by more than 10 percent. Given the current economic environment, this possibility is not welcomed by leaders in New Klowt.

Politically, completion of the dam would be a blow to Emerjant prestige. Emerjant has been clear about its opposition from the moment the proposal was unveiled by Paxony. If Paxony was able to successfully complete the project in the face of Emerjant protest, it would be all the more difficult for Emerjant to claim a spot as a political powerhouse in Politica. In order to earn 5 objective points, Emerjant must prevent Paxony from completing the Grand Kohridor Dam Project.

Minerite

Paxony is a political and economic ally for Minerite, but the Grand Kohridor Dam Project has been a source of tension between the two countries. Much of Minerite's industry sits along the banks of the Kohridor near the city of Mamalode; like Emerjant, there are real concerns that even a small reduction in water flow would have an adverse effect on the Minerite economy. Unlike

Emerjant, however, there is no political incentive to oppose the dams and diversion canals. If anything, Minerite would like Paxony to exact a political victory at the expense of the Emerjants, Industraelites, and Petropoleans. With this in mind, Minerite might be willing to publicly support the project if its negative economic impact were to be mitigated by adequate compensation. If Minerite is able to secure at least 300 resource factors in compensation from Paxony in exchange for public support of the Grand Kohridor Dam Project, it will earn this 5 point objective.

Industrael

Realistically, opposition to the Grand Kohridor Dam Project falls fairly low on Industrael's agenda. In terms of its relationship with Paxony, resolution of the Centralia dispute is much more important to Industrael. The economic impact of the project would be minimal for Industrael; unlike Emerjant and Minerite, Industraelite industrial output would not be significantly damaged. Still, Industrael does not appreciate the heavy-handed approach that Paxony has taken in attempting to garner support on this issue. If for no other reason than to stick it to an old rival, Industrael will continue to do everything it can to keep the project from completion. If it is successful in doing so, it will achieve this 3 point objective.

Refugia

Much like Industrael, Refugia is not interested in getting tangled up in the fight over the Grand Kohridor Dam Project. Issues like nuclear proliferation and the potential genocide in Tundristan are much higher on the Refugee list of priorities. In the end, Refugia actually supports the construction of the dam and diversion canals. Perhaps a reduced water flow will mean that certain shipping traffic will stay away from the Kohridor, opting instead to sail through the Refugee-controlled Zante Straits. If the Grand Kohridor Dam Project is completed, Refugia will net 3 objective points.

Islandia

Islandia does not rely on the Kohridor River as a trade route, or as a symbol of political or religious significance. Islandish—like Refugees—would enjoy the additional leverage that would come along with increased shipping traffic through the Zante Straits, so perhaps completion of the dam is something to look forward to. In order to earn 1 objective point, Islandia needs to ensure that Paxony is able to complete its proposed project.

Tundristan

It does not matter at all to Tundristan if Paxony completes its much-vaunted project. The Tundrek economy is not large enough to worry about transport routes halfway around the world, and the religious significance of the Kohridor River is lost on most Tundreks. Still, Tundristan is upset with the Paxons for positions they have taken in regards to the PTO and the potential investigation of human rights abuses by the PSF. Tundristan will score 1 objective point if it makes life hard for Paxony and prevents the completion of the dam project.

Scenario Outcome Assessment

*Use this space to answer the question your instructor
has provided for this scenario*

Diplomatic Notes

Country Action Report

- Relevant Countries (list all that are involved in action):

1.   5.

2.   6.

3.   7.

4.   8.

- Nature of Action (what are these countries agreeing to do?):

- Required Signatures (majority, including CDM, for democracies; CDM only for others):

	CDM	DIP	ECA	INT	OPP
Paxony					
Refugia					
Emerjant					
Tundristan					
Industrael					
Islandia					
Petropol					
Minerite					

13
Currency Crises

The Emerjant economy has been a model for other growing countries in Politica. Over the past decade, the country has seen foreign investment skyrocket and an amazing increase in exports to a wide range of countries. Because of this economic expansion, Emerjant is now considered one of the most important political players on the global stage. In an era of widespread democratization, the authoritarian regime in the Emerjant capital of New Klowt has enjoyed tremendous popularity because of its economic successes. For a number of years, the Emerjant currency (bai) has been pegged to the always steady Paxon dyme. If the dyme appreciates or depreciates, so does the bai. Because Emerjant had been growing more quickly than Paxony, the bai was considered to be undervalued. This helped fuel Emerjant growth by effectively making their exports less expensive on the international market.

But there are signs of distress showing in the Emerjant economy. Many investors fear that the authoritarian government in New Klowt will hamper long-term growth. Stiffer competition from other growing countries might also eat away at Emerjant's export success. Indeed, Emerjant economic growth has fallen off pace recently—so much so that the bai is now considered to be significantly overvalued. Yet it remains pegged to the Paxon dyme. Investors doubt that the bai will be able to stay pegged to the dyme at the current ratio. If the bai is allowed to trade at the international market rate, its value will undoubtedly fall. With this in mind, foreign investors have started selling off bai-denominated assets and exchanging their bai for more promising currencies. Widespread selling has flooded the international market with bai, placing downward pressure on its value. If the Emerjant government is not able to prop up the bai, its value will collapse and the Emerjant economy will be in ruins. Economic disarray will erase the great power dreams that Emerjant has worked so hard to actualize. There is no way that it can save the bai on its own. Will any other countries be motivated

---

For Further Review: Currency Crises

What caused the Asian financial crisis of 1997? *See* Pierre Richard Agenor, ed., *The Asian Financial Crisis: Causes, Contagion, and Consequences* (Cambridge, UK: Cambridge University Press, 1999).

How do currency crises emerge and spread? How do we stop them? *See* Paul Krugman, *Currency Crises* (Chicago: University of Chicago Press, 2000).

What is the future of currency in international relations? *See* Benjamin Cohen, *The Future of Money* (Princeton, NJ: Princeton University Press, 2003).

---

to prevent the collapse of the Emerjant economy? What measures can be taken to prop up the bai? Could other currencies in Politica suffer a similar fate?

Country Objectives

Emerjant

As the country at the center of an impending currency crisis, Emerjant has the most at stake in this scenario. There is no doubt that the bai is overvalued as currently pegged to the Paxon dyme. But the Emerjant government can ill afford to let its currency float on the international market right now. A panicked sell-off of bai will cause the bottom to fall out of the once strong currency. If this were to happen, the bai would be worthless. Emerjant corporations and families would see their savings disappear overnight and all of the strides Emerjant has made economically in recent years would be for naught. Thus, the Emerjants firmly believe that the only option is to try to prop up the value of the bai by purchasing excess bai off the international market with its reserve stockpiles of foreign currency. If the flood of bai can be stopped, the panic can be eased and the Emerjant economy can be saved.

Unfortunately, Emerjant is quickly running out of cash reserves; it may not be able to purchase the amount of bai necessary to reestablish stability in the currency. In order to prevent the total collapse of the bai, Emerjant needs help from other countries in Politica. If other governments can bail out the Emerjant government with a grant package of 400 factors, it will be able to purchase enough bai to achieve price stability. If Emerjant is able to secure a 400 factor grant from one or more countries in Politica and uses those factors to purchase its own currency off the international market, it will achieve this 10 point objective.

Islandia

As the major foreign investor in Emerjant, Islandia is gravely concerned with the situation there. In Harbur, the belief is that the Emerjant government is solely responsible for the collapse of the bai. Islandish business leaders are frustrated by the lack of economic transparency required by Emerjant leaders in New Klowt and are convinced that those leaders were aware of the warning signs of currency collapse well before they were apparent to outside investors. If the Emerjants would have simply alerted the international community that an economic slowdown were possible, the system would have restored itself to equilibrium without much trouble. Instead, the sudden news of economic downturn in Emerjant triggered a panicked sell-off of bai that has ruined the Emerjant economy and—as a result—cost Islandish investors dearly. Islandia has already been stung by this currency crisis. The last thing it wants to do now is help bail out the irresponsible Emerjant government. Perhaps the best lesson for Emerjant would be to suffer through the current chaos on its own. Islandia will earn 10 points for this objective if it leads the effort to prevent a 400 factor bailout package from being sent to Emerjant.

Industrael

Industrael is scared that the currency crisis in Emerjant could grow large enough to engulf the Industraelite economy. If the collapse of the bai were to drag the Emerjant economy down far enough, the impact would certainly be felt in Industrael. The two countries are not only political allies, they are trading partners. Even with recent advances in Emerjant, the economy there relies heavily on steel and textile imports from Industrael. If demand for these imports were to disappear because of economic collapse in Emerjant, the already troubled industrial sector in Industrael would not be far behind.

There would be a political cost to an Emerjant collapse as well. Emerjant is Industrael's primary ally against the northern coalition of Paxony and Minerite; if it were substantially weakened, Industrael would be left alone to fend off any aggressive behavior from the north. With this is mind, Industrael is intent on helping its neighbor survive this crisis intact. If Industrael is able to help (directly or indirectly) Emerjant receive the 400 factor bailout package necessary to restore stability to the bai, it will achieve this 5 point objective.

Tundristan

Tundristan has not been affected at all by the currency crisis in Emerjant; it has very little economic investment abroad, and is particularly absent from any involvement in the south. Thus, contributing to a massive bailout of the Emerjant government does not seem to make much sense to most Tundreks. After all, the country is having enough problems maintaining a healthy balance sheet itself. Sending money to another country seems even more preposterous when one considers recent news that Islandia, Refugia, and other countries may cease foreign aid shipments to Tundristan in protest of alleged human rights abuses against the Ostracites. Unless Emerjant can somehow guarantee that those foreign aid shipments will not stop, Tundristan has nothing to offer the Emerjants. If Tundristan manages to avoid any involvement in the mess that is the Emerjant currency crisis, it will score 5 objective points.

Petropol

Petropol is reluctant to spend too much time or money saving Emerjant from a mess it brought upon itself, but the facts cannot be ignored—over 20 percent of Petropolean oil exports go to Emerjant. If that market were to dry up, there would be a reduction in demand that would not only cost the Petropoleans in the short run, but also cause the price of oil to drop in the long run. This would be unacceptable. Petropol needs to make sure that Emerjant receives its requested 400 factor bailout package in order to achieve this 3 point objective.

Paxony

Paxon corporations, like their Islandish counterparts, have invested heavily in the Emerjant economy. Insider information helped Paxon investors get out of Emerjant before things got too ugly. Thus, Paxony does not harbor the same ill will toward Emerjant that Islandia does. Even though it sees Emerjant as an emerging competitor in Politica, Paxony is in favor of a bailout package for the Emerjants. If the Emerjant economy collapses, the consequences will spare no one. In Paxony, the consensus is that these negative consequences will outweigh any political benefit that the country will realize from Emerjant's troubles. Paxony will earn 3 points for this objective if Emerjant receives its 400 factor bailout package, but Paxony does not contribute more than 50 of the factors.

Refugia

Very little Refugee goods ever reach Emerjant. An economic collapse there would have no significant impact on the Refugee economy. Like Islandia, most Refugees believe that Emerjant brought this crisis upon itself—maybe it should be left to fend on its own. Refugia does not have a strong position on this issue, so as long as no Refugee factors are included in a bailout package, the country will earn 1 point for this objective.

Minerite

More than any other country, Minerite may have the opportunity to help Emerjant get out of this crisis. Because Emerjant is an important export market for Minerite, there is a strong incentive for Minerite to prevent economic collapse there. Also, the Minerite economy is robust enough to contribute a majority of the 400 factors necessary to bring stability back to the currency and people of Emerjant. The question is: Does Minerite care enough? In order to achieve this 1 point objective, Minerite must make sure that Emerjant gets a 400 factor bail-out package, and that more than 200 factors comes from Minerite itself.

Scenario Outcome Assessment

*Use this space to answer the question your instructor
has provided for this scenario*

Diplomatic Notes

Country Action Report

■ Relevant Countries (list all that are involved in action):

1.   5.

2.   6.

3.   7.

4.   8.

■ Nature of Action (what are these countries agreeing to do?):

■ Required Signatures (majority, including CDM, for democracies; CDM only for others):

	CDM	DIP	ECA	INT	OPP
Paxony					
Refugia					
Emerjant					
Tundristan					
Industrael					
Islandia					
Petropol					
Minerite					

14
Foreign Aid

Thirty years ago, the Tundrek monarchy offered to establish a semiautonomous homeland as a safe haven for the oft-persecuted Ostracite populations in Politica. The move was not entirely altruistic. In return for establishing the Ostracite homeland, Tundristan would receive a large amount of foreign aid on an annual basis from countries with sizeable Ostracite populations, like Refugia and Islandia. Other developed countries such as Paxony and Minerite have also sent varying amounts of aid to Tundristan on numerous occasions. This aid has contributed greatly to industrial development and social programs in Tundristan over the years. Although the country is still far from prosperous, the progress it has made would have been impossible without the influx of foreign aid.

Today, there is talk of discontinuing the aid program to Tundristan, or at least attaching more conditions to it. First and foremost, Islandia and Refugia are upset about the alleged human rights abuses that may be taking place in the semiautonomous Ostracite homeland. These two countries argue that while the Tundrek monarchy should be commended for opening its doors to the Ostracites in the first place, it is no longer looking out for their best interests. In the minds of both Islandia and Refugia, the only way to improve the situation in Tundristan is for the monarch to step down and allow for the emergence of a representative democracy that will include a voice for the Ostracites. Unless the Tundreks declare a self-imposed transition to democratic rule, Islandia and Refugia will withdraw the foreign aid that has been so crucial to Tundristan's stability. Other countries have joined in, arguing that additional strings be attached to foreign aid. Minerite and Paxony, for example, have suggested that they will cut their foreign aid to Tundristan unless the Tundreks agree to make the necessary structural adjustments to their economy for them to qualify to join the PTO. Not all states are in favor of such a heavy-handed approach to Tundristan. Petropol, for example, has described the current scenario as an example of "international

---

For Further Review: Foreign Aid

Does foreign aid solve the problems it is supposed to? *See* Robert Caldersi, *The Trouble with Africa: Why Foreign Aid Isn't Working* (New York: Palgrave, 2006).

What are the motivations of donor countries when it comes to foreign aid? *See* David Halloran Lumsdaine, *Moral Vision in International Politics: The Foreign Aid Regime, 1949–1989* (Princeton, NJ: Princeton University Press, 1993).

Why do some countries get more foreign aid than others? *See* Alberto Alesina and David Dollar, "Who Gives Foreign Aid to Whom and Why?" *Journal of Economic Growth* 5, no. 1 (2000): 33–63.

---

bullying" while Industrael calls the international demands placed on Tundristan "a destruction of sovereignty." Will Tundristan accept the conditions that are attached to the foreign aid it depends on? What right do states like Islandia and Refugia have to back out of a long-standing agreement just because they disagree with Tundristan's domestic politics? Can a compromise be reached?

Country Objectives

Tundristan

The ruling elites in Wasibad know that Tundristan would be in shambles without the foreign aid it receives on a yearly basis from countries like Islandia, Refugia, Minerite, and Paxony. The monarchy is willing to go to great lengths to make sure that all current foreign aid programs continue without interruption. But the recent demands of regime change from Islandia and Refugia and economic restructuring from Minerite and Paxony seem way too excessive. Since when should outside forces be able to dictate the domestic politics of another country simply because they have control over the purse strings of Politica? Tundristan recognizes international concern regarding the conflict with ethnic Ostracites in the west of the country, but government officials maintain that Tundristan is the victim in the conflict, not the criminal. If anything, the monarch has shown great patience by not ordering immediate retaliation after recent suicide bombing conducted by militant, pro-independence Ostracite organizations. A populist, democratically elected government would have a hard time showing similar restraint. Democratization is not the answer—it will just cause more instability and subject the Ostracites to persecution from the ethnic

Tundrek majority. And if Islandia and Refugia were to cut off their aid shipments to Tundristan, the economic breakdown of Tundristan would very likely result in a full-scale civil war between the Ostracites and ethnic Tundreks.

Likewise, calls for economic restructuring are understood by Tundristan, but the timing is just not right. In the long run, Tundristan would like to be an open participant in the global market, but until some domestic industries are improved and the situation with the Ostracites is resolved, the Tundrek economy is simply not in position to compete on a level playing field. Forcing Tundristan to join the PTO would be like passing a death sentence on the Tundrek economy. Withholding foreign aid to punish Tundristan's nonparticipation would have a similar effect. To achieve this 10 point objective, Tundristan must convince Islandia, Refugia, Minerite, and Paxony to continue their foreign aid shipments without giving into demands for democratization or economic restructuring and membership in the PTO.

Refugia

Refugia refuses to be fooled by the rhetoric coming out of Wasibad. The Tundrek monarchy is intent on maintaining political power and the wealth it has enjoyed as a result of the foreign aid that streams into the country. Refugee intelligence reports have concluded that less than 20 percent of foreign aid actually makes it into the general population, and less than 2 percent goes to the Ostracite population in Tundristan. Regime change is the only answer in Tundristan, and unless the monarchy agrees to a new democratic government that includes a voice for the Ostracites, Refugia will not send another penny. In the absence of democratization, it will also do everything it can to stop all foreign aid to Tundristan. Refugia will earn 10 objective points if it is able to convince Tundristan to agree to democratize or—in the absence of regime change—it signs a CAR that officially stops all foreign aid to Tundristan.

Paxony

The calls for regime change coming from Refugia (and Islandia as well) are a bit too harsh. How can the rest of Politica expect the existing government in Wasibad to simply step aside because they are asked to do so? There is no need for regime change in Tundristan, just as there is no need for an independent state for the Ostracites. Both developments would be too damaging to the stability that Paxony has fought so hard to establish in Politica. But, Paxony is interested in economic reform in Tundristan. Many of the recent problems in that country can be traced to the failings of the closed economy. Paxony is willing to continue sending aid to help the social and political stability of Tundristan, but only under the condition of significant economic reform. This reform would be accomplished if Tundristan agreed to join the PTO. If Paxony is able to convince Tundristan to do so, it will earn 5 objective points.

Petropol

Tundristan is being held hostage via a strategy of economic blackmail. As a strong ally of the Tundreks, Petropol is not willing to stand by and allow a few pompous countries to press their political and economic agendas at the expense of the Tundreks. If Refugia and its lapdogs decide to cease existing foreign aid shipments to Tundristan because of petty grievances, Petropol will make them pay. The countries in question—particularly Paxony and Islandia—should remember that oil shipments can be shut off just as easily as foreign aid shipments. Of course, Petropol would rather not have to resort to such extreme measures as an oil embargo. In order to achieve this 5 point objective, Petropol must make sure that at least two of the existing four donor states (Refugia, Islandia, Paxony, and Minerite) continue existing foreign aid programs in Tundristan.

Islandia

Islandish have just about had it with the Tundrek monarchy. Time after time, the government has lied through its teeth in order to avoid international condemnation on human rights abuses. Now, the government is lying to ensure that foreign aid continues to pour into the country. Enough is enough. Islandia joins Refugia in identifying regime change as a prerequisite for continued foreign aid. Unless the monarchy in Wasibad steps aside to allow for a democratically elected government, Islandia will cease all aid at once. Islandia can achieve this 3 point objective by achieving regime change in Tundristan or—in the absence of regime change—ceasing all foreign aid to that country.

Minerite

Minerite would love to see economic reform in Tundristan, but forcing the government to step aside is too drastic a measure. From a selfish standpoint, the instability (even civil war) that might accompany regime change would likely have an adverse effect on Minerite itself. In the past, political instability in Tundristan has caused an influx of refugees across the Pella Canal and into Minerite. Refugees are not cheap to take care of. Minerite is reluctant to cut off foreign aid to Tundristan. As long as the monarchy promises to enact political reforms and consider PTO membership in the near future, Minerite will keep the aid flowing. If Minerite can convince Paxony, Refugia, and Islandia to adopt this approach (continued aid in return for a promise to reform) it will achieve 3 objective points.

Industrael

What the northern countries do with their money is their own business, but Industrael refuses to stand by and let the likes of Refugia and Paxony bully a potential ally like Tundristan. The donor countries have a legal obligation to continue aid shipments. Simple suspicion and dislike for Tundristan's economic policies are not enough to warrant the withdrawal from this obligation. Industrael will score 1 objective point if at least two of the donor countries continue their existing foreign aid programs in Tundristan.

Emerjant

Tundristan is a potential ally—Emerjant hopes that they will join the just-formed NPB, which is headquartered in New Klowt. Political motivations alone are sufficient to draw Emerjant to Tundristan's side when it comes to questions of foreign aid. Although Emerjant itself is not in a position to offer economic assistance, it will achieve 1 objective point if at least two of the four donor countries continue their existing foreign aid programs in Tundristan.

Scenario Outcome Assessment

*Use this space to answer the question your instructor
has provided for this scenario*

Diplomatic Notes

Country Action Report

■ Relevant Countries (list all that are involved in action):

1.   5.

2.   6.

3.   7.

4.   8.

■ Nature of Action (what are these countries agreeing to do?):

■ Required Signatures (majority, including CDM, for democracies; CDM only for others):

	CDM	DIP	ECA	INT	OPP
Paxony					
Refugia					
Emerjant					
Tundristan					
Industrael					
Islandia					
Petropol					
Minerite					

15
Global Security Organizations

In the aftermath of the last Great Paxon-Industraelite War, it was decided by victorious and defeated powers alike that a global organization was needed to promote peace and stability in Politica. Thus, as part of the peace settlement that marked the end of that war, the Politican Security Forum was established. The five-member forum includes three permanent members—Paxony, Industrael, and Islandia. The two remaining members are selected on a rotating schedule from the other states in Politica. Presently, the two nonpermanent members are Tundristan and Refugia. While all members have a vote in deciding PSF policies, the three permanent members have the power to veto any action or policy. Veto power was given to both Paxony and Industrael to ensure that there was a balanced agenda at the PSF. Islandia was included as a neutral power in order to make sure that the PSF was not hijacked by the two superpower states.

Over the years, the PSF has been successful in some areas and unsuccessful in others. It has played a crucial role in facilitating the arms reduction treaties signed by Paxony and Industrael in the postwar years. It has also served as an important mediator in settling interstate disputes. On several occasions, the PSF has prevented the escalation of conflict between the Petropoleans and ethnic Ostracites in Refugia. In two separate instances, the PSF has kept the Tundreks and Refugees from going to war over the closure of the Zante Straits. Presently, the PSF is contemplating an investigation into alleged human rights abuses by the Tundrek government in the semiautonomous Ostracite homeland.

But some states believe that the PSF could be even more effective if it were restructured to better represent the modern-day political situation in Politica. While Paxony, Industrael, and Islandia are important powers today, they are no longer so dominant on the global stage. Paxony has taken a step away from active leadership, Industrael is in decay, and Islandia has focused more on commercial pursuits. Other countries have stepped in to fill the leadership gap;

For Further Review: Global Security Organizations

How is the United Nations Security Council changing? *See* Bruce Russett, ed., *The Once and Future Security Council* (New York: St. Martin's, 1997).

Will the United Nations Security Council be reformed? Does it matter? *See* Thomas G. Weiss, "The Illusion of United Nations Security Council Reform," *Washington Quarterly* 26, no. 4 (2003): 147–161.

How do countries signal their satisfaction or dissatisfaction with the international system with votes in the United Nations Security Council? *See* Steve S. Chan, "A Poisson Analysis of UN Security Council Vetoes," *Cooperation and Conflict* 38 (2003): 339–359.

Minerite, Emerjant, and Petropol all have great power ambitions. Perhaps one or more of these countries should be added as a permanent, veto-wielding member of the PSF. But which country or countries is most deserving of a position that demands so much responsibility? Some argue that the PSF is better served by remaining as is, while others agree that restructuring is necessary but disagree on how drastic that restructuring should be. One thing is certain—the new balance of power in Politica could be decided by the changes made to the PSF. Selection as a permanent member requires the vote of all three existing permanent members and at least one additional vote from a nonpermanent member.

Country Objectives

Minerite

If there are any additions made to the permanent membership on the PSF, Minerite feels that it deserves to be one of the countries added. As a growing country with a stable democratic tradition and a strong military, Minerite has already shown a great deal of responsibility in the international community. It is a net donor when it comes to foreign aid and it is a proponent of other international organizations such as the PTO. It has even agreed to consider joining the proposed Politican Court of Justice. Compared to the other candidates for permanent membership (Emerjant and Petropol), Minerite is economically stable and politically liberal. All in all, Minerites would argue that their value system is much more in line with that of most Politicans than is the value system found in Emerjant or Petropol.

For Minerite, permanent membership on the PSF would symbolize its emergence as a great power on equal footing with the likes of Paxony, Industrael, and

Islandia. Coupled with its leadership position in the NPTO, veto power on the PSF may just make Minerite the most influential state in Politica. In order to achieve this 10 point objective, Minerite must secure permanent membership on the PSF and make sure that—at most—only one of the other two candidates is also selected as a new permanent member.

Petropol

Petropol's economic leverage in Politica is well known. With so much of Politica's oil, it is hard to ignore the power that Petropol enjoys when negotiating with other countries on any issue of economic, political, or social importance. Still, the rest of Politica has been slow to recognize Petropol as a prime time player when it comes to politics. Perhaps the traditionalism of Petropolean society or its geographic isolation has kept it from achieving the recognition it deserves. Regardless, the debate over the restructuring of the PSF allows Petropol the perfect chance to take a step into the inner circle of great powers from which it has been excluded for so long.

For other states in Politica, selecting Petropol as a permanent member of the PSF makes sense in terms of balancing the political stance of the forum to better represent the interests of both the north and south. The Petropolean candidacy should be particularly attractive to "outsider" states like Tundristan. Perhaps the Petropoleans could serve as a voice of reason in the PSF when the pro-Ostracite states of Islandia, Refugia, and Paxony begin to push their agenda on the Tundreks. Petropol's goal is simply that of inclusion. Regardless of which other countries are or are not selected as permanent members of the PSF, Petropol will earn 10 objective points if it is chosen.

Emerjant

Emerjant is the dark horse candidate for a permanent seat on the PSF; this is particularly the case given the recent economic troubles it has been experiencing. Still, Emerjant is an attractive candidate due to its general trend toward economic expansion. Some states may support the Emerjant candidacy because it would balance out what some see as the skewed political perspective of the PSF. With Paxony and Islandia always pushing for free trade and democracy, perhaps the four nondemocracies in Politica would prefer to see authoritarian Emerjant given permanent membership instead of liberal Minerite.

For Emerjant, permanent membership would bring a plethora of benefits. First and foremost, selection would convey the kind of political prestige that it has been so desperately seeking. In addition, a permanent voice on the PSF would ensure that Emerjant concerns (like the emerging currency crisis) were more likely to receive global attention. With this in mind, Emerjant will earn 5 objective points if it is selected for permanent membership. Other selections (Petropol or Minerite) have no effect on Emerjant's success.

Islandia

Islandia is firmly against any additional permanent members of the PSF. The current structure, with Paxony and Industrael balancing each other and Islandia as a politically neutral voice, has worked perfectly fine over the decades. Adding new permanent members with veto power may render the PSF incapable of action in any scenario. It will be next to impossible to achieve any consensus with four, five, or six veto-wielding powers. In the interest of preserving the PSF as a viable actor, the Islandish will use their existing veto power to prevent the addition of new permanent members. If they are successful in doing so, they will earn 5 objective points.

Industrael

The idea of expanding the PSF is an attractive one for Industrael. It was the primary proponent in opening the debate in the first place. The first priority for the Industraelites is to add balance to the group of permanent members. On a number of occasions, Industrael has been isolated by consensus between Paxony and Islandia. While Industrael has not been afraid to use its veto power in such situations, doing so comes at a certain political cost. Having an alternative voice as a permanent member of the PSF would take some of the pressure off of Industrael. It will achieve this 3 point objective if either Petropol or Emerjant (or both) are selected as permanent members of the PSF.

Paxony

Even though it enjoys having leverage (along with Islandia) in the PSF given the current format, Paxony is open to a number of different restructuring plans. In general, the Paxons are looking to step back a bit from their leadership position in Politica. Why not let someone else take on some of the burden Paxony has shouldered for so long? The only development Paxony would oppose is the selection of both Petropol and Emerjant and the exclusion of Minerite. Such an outcome would bring about an unacceptable shift in the political perspective of the PSF. Other than this outcome, however, Paxony supports any combination of new permanent members and will achieve this 3 point objective when expansion occurs.

Refugia

Despite its status as a nonpermanent member, Refugia has little or no interest in the PSF. It has worked well in the past, but its recent reluctance to act aggressively to investigate potential human rights abuses in Tundristan has convinced the Refugees that the PSF is a lost cause. Refugia's only concern would be if Petropol were selected as a permanent member of the PSF. Petropol's anti-Ostracite agenda would then be granted a certain amount of international legitimacy. As long as Petropol is prevented from becoming a permanent member of the PSF, Refugia will achieve this 1 point objective.

Tundristan

Like Refugia, Tundristan does not put a lot of faith in the PSF. In the past and in the present, the PSF has done nothing but cause the Tundreks grief. Let them restructure however they want—the PSF will still have it in for Tundristan. The only ray of hope might be the selection of Tundristan's ally Petropol as a permanent member. If this were to occur, Tundristan would earn 1 objective point.

Scenario Outcome Assessment

*Use this space to answer the question your instructor
has provided for this scenario*

Diplomatic Notes

Country Action Report

■ **Relevant Countries** (list all that are involved in action):

1.   5.

2.   6.

3.   7.

4.   8.

■ **Nature of Action** (what are these countries agreeing to do?):

■ **Required Signatures** (majority, including CDM, for democracies; CDM only for others):

	CDM	DIP	ECA	INT	OPP
Paxony					
Refugia					
Emerjant					
Tundristan					
Industrael					
Islandia					
Petropol					
Minerite					

16

International Criminal Courts

In response to the atrocities committed during the last Great Paxon-Industraelite War, a war crimes tribunal was established in Berg in order to try a number of Industraelite military commanders for crimes against humanity. A number of high profile cases resulted in executions. Industrael has always maintained that the tribunal was a classic example of power determining justice; had Industrael emerged victorious in the conflict, it would have been Paxon generals that were sentenced to death. Was Paxony's decision to detonate a nuclear bomb on its own soil not a war crime in itself?

The debate over the legitimacy of the Berg War Crimes Tribunal is still in progress, but recent atrocities and the desire to increase a sense of collective justice in Politica has led to much discussion about the creation of a nonpartisan, Politican Court of Justice (PCJ). The PCJ would have universal jurisdiction in all member states when it came to identifying and trying crimes against humanity such as genocide or torture. Individuals could be extradited and tried at PCJ headquarters. Decisions by the PCJ, and accompanying sentences, would be binding for all members.

On the surface, the PCJ seems rather noncontroversial. There are no states in Politica that would oppose universal jurisdiction in undisputed cases of genocide, torture, or other crimes against humanity. But oftentimes it is hard to get multiple parties to agree on the status of a particular act as a crime against humanity. Alleged victims may exaggerate their claim (if they are still alive) and the accused may never admit that their behavior is eligible for trial at the PCJ. Thus, the notion of sovereignty comes into play. Are countries in Politica willing to cede a certain amount of sovereignty to universal jurisdiction? What if the PCJ takes on a political agenda and certain member states are unfairly targeted? Is the sense of collective justice really worth the loss of sovereign immunity?

For Further Review: International Criminal Courts

What is the appropriate balance to strike between national sovereignty and international justice? *See* William Driscoll, William Zompetti, and Suzette Zompetti, eds., *The International Criminal Court: Global Politics and the Quest for Justice* (New York: IDEA, 2004).

Will the United States ever join the International Criminal Court? *See* Sarah B. Sewall and Carl Kaysen, eds., *The United States and the International Criminal Court* (Lanham, MD: Rowman & Littlefield, 2000).

When does universal jurisdiction trump sovereign immunity? *See* Reed Brody and Michael Ratner, eds., *The Pinochet Papers: The Case of Augusto Pinochet in Spain and Britain* (The Hague: Kluwer International, 2000).

Country Objectives

Paxony

Paxons are convinced that no state has suffered more from crimes against humanity than it has; the atrocities perpetrated by the Industraelites during their invasion of Paxony are too unspeakable to mention here. With these memories fresh in their hearts and minds, Paxons have taken the initiative when it comes to establishing the PCJ. The Paxons propose that the court be headquartered in Berg and use the same facilities that were constructed to host the controversial Berg War Crimes Tribunal. Of course all states in Politica would be welcome to join, as long as they understand that—once established—the concept of universal jurisdiction will override that of sovereign immunity when dealing with potential crimes against humanity. Political leaders in member states will be subject to extradition and trial in Berg if they are charged with acts of genocide, torture, political assassination, and other specific crimes yet to be decided. For Paxony, the loss of sovereign immunity that would come with membership in the PCJ is well worth the construction of an international organization that will help prevent the recurrence of atrocities such as those that occurred during the last Paxon-Industraelite War. In order to achieve 10 objective points, Paxony must convince at least five other states to join the PCJ, and ensure that the PCJ is headquartered in Berg.

Tundristan

The much-trumpeted concept of collective justice is a sham. Paxony and other states are pushing for an international criminal court simply so they can further their own political agendas. Tundreks are convinced that the Berg War Crimes Tribunal was just another example of the ancient revelation that "might makes right." While Industrael was surely guilty of horrendous acts during its war with Paxony, its behavior was no more abhorrent than Paxony's. War is a messy enterprise, and the notion of war crimes is just a tool of revenge for those that emerge victorious.

International attitudes about the current conflict between the Tundrek government and its Ostracite population illustrate the fickle nature of collective justice. While Tundristan is castigated for using violence to prevent revolution, the world turns a blind eye to the ruthless suicide bombings used by the Ostracites to kill innocent Tundrek civilians. If the PCJ is established, there is no doubt that its first act will be to charge brave Tundrek soldiers with crimes against humanity. In reality, any violence that has taken place in Tundristan is largely the result of the increasingly outrageous acts by a small and aggressive group of pro-independence groups based in the Ostracite homeland. Tundristan's objective is to minimize membership in the PCJ. If fewer than five countries join the court, Tundristan will earn 10 objective points.

Refugia

In the grand scheme of things, a strong PCJ would be much more successful in protecting the Ostracite people than the unreliable PSF. In addition to raising awareness about the plight of persecuted peoples around the world, the PCJ might also be successful in actually punishing those that are guilty of the persecution. Refugia is very much in favor of the PCJ, but given the problems associated with the earlier Berg War Crimes Tribunal, Paxony should not serve as the court's headquarters. The beautiful coastal city of Sansafe is a much more appropriate location for the PCJ. If Refugia and four or more other states join the PCJ, and the headquarters of the court are in Sansafe, Refugia will earn 5 objective points.

Petropol

Once again, Petropol finds that its interests are aligned with those of Tundristan; the Petropoleans oppose the formation of the PCJ. The court is simply a tool that will be used to unfairly punish the Tundreks for crimes they have not committed. The agenda of the PCJ will be dominated by states with a concept of justice that is entirely out of line with that found in Petropol. If it joins such an organization, Petropol will have modernity and progress shoved down its throat. Without question, Petropol opposes the PCJ. If it refuses to join and convinces three other states to similarly abstain, Petropol will earn 5 objective points.

Islandia

Islandia is a strong supporter of a PCJ. Regardless of its location, the PCJ will be the first step toward a more secure world where states can focus on economic and social prosperity rather than political differences. By creating a sense of collective justice, the PCJ will help to erase the borders that have divided Politica for so long. Perhaps the long-term result will be the elimination of systematic violence as a social phenomenon. While the first item on the PCJ agenda should be the alleged war crimes in Tundristan, it is important that countries like Tundristan do not perceive the PCJ as a political tool to be used against them. In that spirit, Islandia is intent on convincing at least one so-called outsider country to join the PCJ. Regardless of total membership in the PCJ, Islandia will earn 3 objective points if (in addition to joining the PCJ itself) it can convince either Tundristan or Petropol to join the court.

Minerite

While Minerite supports the principle of the PCJ, it does not feel that Politica is quite ready to choose universal jurisdiction over sovereign immunity. For one thing, a number of Minerite soldiers were recently arrested for sexual assault while on leave in Refugia. The Refugees were determined to try the Minerites in Sansafe under the Refugee judicial system, but Minerite fought long and hard to bring the soldiers back to Mamalode and grant them trial in a Minerite military court. Because of instances such as this, Minerite is reluctant to grant too much power to an international court. Minerite might support the PCJ in a decade or so, but not today. If Minerite abstains from joining the PCJ, it will earn 3 objective points.

Industrael

Despite its bad experience at the hands of the Paxons during the Berg War Crimes Tribunal, Industrael is not opposed to the establishment of an international court. If a PCJ were to exist, however, it would have to be truly nonpartisan. That means that Industrael would only join the PCJ if at least one of its political friends (Emerjant, Petropol, or Tundristan) were also to join. If Industrael joins the PCJ along with at least one of the three states listed above, it will earn 1 objective point.

Emerjant

Like Industrael, Emerjant is only interested in a PCJ that would represent the interests of all member states. Joining the court would be another symbol of the political prestige that Emerjant hungers for, but the PCJ would only truly be legitimate if Emerjant were able to convince Industrael, Petropol, or Tundristan to join as well. If Emerjant joins, and is successful in convincing at least one of the three states listed above to do the same, it will earn 1 objective point.

Scenario Outcome Assessment

*Use this space to answer the question your instructor
has provided for this scenario*

Diplomatic Notes

Country Action Report

■ Relevant Countries (list all that are involved in action):

1.   5.

2.   6.

3.   7.

4.   8.

■ Nature of Action (what are these countries agreeing to do?):

■ Required Signatures (majority, including CDM, for democracies; CDM only for others):

	CDM	DIP	ECA	INT	OPP
Paxony					
Refugia					
Emerjant					
Tundristan					
Industrael					
Islandia					
Petropol					
Minerite					

17
Collective Action Problems

While accurate information is hard to come by, initial reports out of southern Industrael indicate that there has been an outbreak of the Bovine Fever. The Bovine Fever has shown up in human populations on a number of occasions over the past century, but this is the first time that the virus has shown signs of being easily transmitted through airborne particles. Interviews with infected patients imply that the virus is being spread from human to human with very minimal contact. The prognosis for outbreak containment is not good. A number of Industraelite villages have been quarantined, but there are fears that the Bovine Fever has already spread outside the quarantine zone. If the virus reaches a major city or—worse yet—a transportation hub, the result might be a global pandemic of unprecedented lethality.

Still, it is not too late to take action. Small stockpiles of an effective vaccine already exist. An enlarged quarantine area, careful treatment of those already infected, and aggressive vaccine production would likely limit the consequences of the current Bovine Fever outbreak. But Industrael cannot take action alone. The human and material costs of preventing a pandemic are enormous. A number of estimates put the overall cost of containing the Bovine Fever outbreak at 1,200 factors. If Politican countries are able to come together and allocate the necessary factors, scientists are certain that the outbreak will be contained. If the international community fails to come up with the necessary 1,200 factors, the Bovine Fever will have its way with much of the world.

The challenge, then, is to decide how the 1,200 factors will be collected. Should certain countries shoulder more of the burden than others? Is it the responsibility of the rich to act in times like this, or should the countries that stand to lose the most be compelled to contribute a majority of the required factors? What about countries that will not be affected at all? With disaster at hand, Politicans must put aside their differences and work together in order to stop the Bovine Fever from spreading.

For Further Review: Collective Action Problems
Why is it so hard for groups to act collectively to provide public goods? *See* Mancur Olson, *The Logic of Collective Action: Public Goods and the Theory of Groups* (Cambridge, MA: Harvard University Press, 1965).
Is collective action even possible on a global scale? *See* Todd Sandler, *Global Collective Action* (Cambridge, UK: Cambridge University Press, 2004).
Will the avian flu turn into a global pandemic? *See* Laurie Garrett, "The Next Pandemic?" *Foreign Affairs* 84, no. 4 (2005): 3–23.

Country Objectives

Industrael

Industrael is ground zero for the Bovine Fever outbreak. There are already hundreds of fatalities and thousands more infected, but there is still a chance to minimize the impact of this disaster. If, however, the international community fails to generate the 1,200 factors necessary to contain the outbreak, Industrael will be forever changed. Industrael has a lot at stake: if the Bovine Fever can be contained, Industrael will earn 10 objective points.

Emerjant

Because Emerjant is Industrael's neighbor, ally, and trading partner, chances are that the Bovine Fever has already crossed the border and infected at least one unlucky Emerjant. Still, the time to act for Emerjant is now. If the outbreak can somehow be contained, Emerjant will earn 10 objective points.

Minerite

Current projections put Minerite right in the path of the spreading Bovine Fever outbreak. From Industrael, most transportation routes funnel traffic right into the Minerite capital of Mamalode. There is no time to waste for Minerite. If the outbreak is contained, Minerite will earn 5 objective points.

Paxony

Like Minerite, Paxony would quickly feel the effects of a global pandemic. As the crossroads of Politican civilization, it is impossible for Paxony to secure its porous borders. Therefore, Paxony is very interested in making sure that the fever is limited to the already-affected Industraelite villages. If the outbreak is contained, Paxony will earn 5 objective points.

Refugia

There is little doubt that the close-knit Refugee society would be devastated by a global pandemic. Traditional customs discourage the Ostracites from seeking medical attention, and containing an outbreak once it got to Refugia would be next to impossible. Thus, Refugia has a strong incentive to stop the outbreak now. If the virus is successfully contained, Refugia will achieve this objective and earn 3 objective points.

Tundristan

Tundristan is a relatively isolated state. Because it already limits foreign commercial traffic and is only attached to the rest of Politica via the narrow Pella Isthmus, there is a reasonable chance that Tundristan can escape the wrath of the Bovine Fever. That said, if the virus does reach Tundristan, domestic chaos will likely prevent the government from successfully managing an outbreak. If the outbreak is contained in Industrael, Tundristan will score 3 objective points.

Islandia

As the only island state in Politica, Islandia is uniquely situated to avoid the worst of the Bovine Fever outbreak. Even if the virus is unchecked, tight border controls and the highly advanced Islandish health care system would minimize its potential impact on Islandia. The stakes just are not that high for Islandia, but it will still earn 1 objective point if the outbreak is contained.

Petropol

Petropol's geographic isolation will come in handy when it comes to surviving a global pandemic. The Islandia desert separates the bulk of Petopolean society from Industrael and the rest of Politica. The closed nature of Petropolean society also minimizes the country's vulnerability. Still, no outbreak is better than a small one; Petropol will earn 1 objective point if the Bovine Fever outbreak is contained.

Scenario Outcome Assessment
Use this space to answer the question your instructor
has provided for this scenario

Diplomatic Notes

Country Action Report

■ **Relevant Countries** (list all that are involved in action):

1.   5.

2.   6.

3.   7.

4.   8.

■ **Nature of Action** (what are these countries agreeing to do?):

■ **Required Signatures** (majority, including CDM, for democracies; CDM only for others):

	CDM	DIP	ECA	INT	OPP
Paxony					
Refugia					
Emerjant					
Tundristan					
Industrael					
Islandia					
Petropol					
Minerite					

18
Environmental Challenges

After traveling to the highest reaches of Mount Oros (Politica's tallest peak) in the uninhabited region of Milos, an international expedition has brought back alarming reports of retreating glaciers, melting ice sheets, and unprecedented warming. Along the once-frigid northern coast of Milos, recent summers have been warm enough to decrease ice content by up to 35 percent and increase the flow of the wild Gursu River by over 75 percent. Environmental changes have not been restricted to this remote southern region of Politica. In the north, Tundrek officials have reported the lowest snow pack in recorded history. The Drama Mountains in eastern Minerite, once filled with stunning glaciers, are essentially ice-free for six months out of the year. Even in the heart of Politica, the global environment seems to be changing drastically. Rainfall is up markedly in the Paxon heartland, and the average yearly temperature in Berg was the highest ever. Interestingly, just a couple hundred miles to the east in Industrael, farmers are facing a sixth year of drought. The last three cyclone seasons in Refugia and Islandia have set all-time records for intensity and destruction. The level of the Placidic Sea—both north and south—has risen almost a foot in under a decade.

The Politican environment is changing, there is no doubt. The question remains: What is responsible for this change? Are human industrial activities and carbon dioxide emissions the primary culprits, or are recent changes just part of the normal variance that one can expect in a complex ecological system? If Politicans are responsible for the changing environment, what can be done to halt this change, or at least reduce its progress?

A group of states most affected by environmental change (Refugia, Emerjant, and Tundristan) have drafted the Wasibad Protocol on Climate Change (WPCC). After a meeting in the Tundrek capital last year, these three states came to a consensus that, in all likelihood, human carbon emissions were a primary culprit in causing the drastic environmental changes that Politican scientists have been

---

For Further Review: Environmental Challenges

Will we always ruin our common resources? *See* Garrett Hardin, "The Tragedy of the Commons," *Science* 162 (1968): 1243–1248.

Why have some countries found the Kyoto Protocol difficult to follow? *See* David G. Victor, *The Collapse of the Kyoto Protocol and the Struggle to Stop Global Warming* (Princeton, NJ: Princeton University Press, 2001).

Want a thorough overview of the environmental challenges facing the world? *See* Gareth Porter, Janet Welsh Brown, and Pamela S. Chasek, *Global Environmental Politics* (Boulder, CO: Westview Press, 2000).

---

recording in recent decades. With human carbon emissions increasing at over 15 percent per year, the WPCC forecasts even more startling changes in the future. While it is certainly possible for Politican societies to adapt to a new environment, the economic, social, and political trauma of the adaptation process is impossible to ponder. In an effort to prevent a worst case scenario of global climate change, the WPCC calls for each country in Politica to eliminate increases in carbon emissions during the next decade and then begin to reduce those emissions by up to 40 percent in the ensuing 40 years. Dubbed the "40/40 Plan," the WPCC would necessitate massive changes in the everyday life of most Politicans. Some analysts worry that the economic impact of the 40/40 Plan will cause more trauma than the worst case scenario of climate change. To achieve the transformations outlined by the plan, industrialized states (Paxony, Islandia, Industrael, and Minerite) would have to allocate 450 factors each to revamping their industry, energy, and transportation sectors. Less developed countries (Refugia, Emerjant, Tundristan, and Petropol) would need to allocate 150 factors each in order to make sure upcoming development takes place within the guidelines of the WPCC. For Politica as a whole, the cost of successfully implementing the WPCC is a whopping 2,400 factors. If any of the eight countries fails to allocate the factors it needs in order to adhere to the 40/40 Plan, the WPCC will be worthless and the situation in Politica will—quite literally—heat up in no time.

Country Objectives

Refugia

Refugee society is dependent on the health of the Placidic Sea. Excessively warm waters are not conducive to a large fish catch. More importantly, rising sea levels threaten to inundate much of the low-lying coastal lands that comprise the already small country. There are already signs that damage to the Placidic Sea may be irreversible, but it would be a crime for Refugia to simply give up and throw its hands into the air. As it has been from the start, Refugia is a firm supporter of the WPCC. In fact, the government in Sansafe has made it a national security priority second only to safeguarding the Ostracites in Tundristan. Refugia does not have a large industrial sector to reform, or bad societal habits that must be changed. But even if it did, no cost would be too high when it comes to mitigating global climate change. Refugia will gladly allocate its share of 150 factors to signing the WPCC and adhere to the 40/40 Plan. If the other seven countries in Politica join Refugia in conforming to the requirements of the WPCC and the 40/40 Plan, it will earn 10 points for this objective.

Islandia

No country is in support of massive global climate change. Islandia's southern coast has already been affected by a severe cyclone season and slightly rising sea levels. But is there anything Politicans can really do to stop it? Without question, the proposed 40/40 Plan is not the answer. The plan is too expensive and it is unjust—why should industrialized countries be asked to shoulder so much of the burden? Is it fair for lesser developed countries like Tundristan to claim that the rich have a right to send foreign aid their way, but then also penalize those rich countries for the industrial might that allows them to send that aid? Islandia is a highly advanced economy that is working on its own to make its society more eco-friendly. Islandia is willing to help out with global efforts to control climate change, but the 40/40 Plan is uncertain in its outcome and exorbitant in cost. Islandia is not opposed to signing the WPCC, but it will only achieve this 10 point objective if it refuses to spend more than 200 factors on adhering to the conditions of the plan.

Industrael

Signing the WPCC and adhering to the 40/40 Plan would be a disaster for the Industraelite economy. It is no secret that Industrael has a large number of coal, steel, and textile factories that emit heavy doses of carbon into the atmosphere. This has been the case for the past century, and it will continue to be the case until the Industraelite economy modernizes. But Industrael cannot worry about the potential climate change somewhere down the road when it has jobs and industrial output to worry about right now. Drought in the agricultural north is nothing compared to revolution throughout the entire country. Industrael agrees to the WPCC in principle and is not opposed to signing in 10 or 20 years. But now is not the time. In order to achieve this 5 point objective, Industrael must not sign the WPCC or allocate any factors toward adherence to the 40/40 Plan.

Tundristan

More than any other country, Tundristan has quite a bit to lose when it comes to global climate change. Melting ice fields in the north will bring flooding to villages and destroy the regional tourist industry while rising seas in the south will spell disaster for many large and influential coastal communities. With such high stakes, Tundristan has taken a leading role in pushing for passage of the WPCC and adherence to the 40/40 Plan. It is more than willing to allocate 150 factors (or more) to meet the challenge, and it is hoping that other countries will follow its example. Unfortunately, ongoing disputes with several states mean that Tundrek credibility is at an all-time low. Maybe Tundristan can use the issue of climate change to foster warmer relations between itself and the rest of Politica. If the WPCC is signed by all eight countries, and each of the eight allocates the necessary factors to adhere to the 40/40 Plan, Tundristan will achieve this 5 point objective.

Emerjant

The current economic situation in Emerjant is not as favorable as it was five years ago. A looming currency crisis and general decline in exports make this a bad time for additional expenditures in areas like climate change prevention. But the consequences of climate change have already been felt along much of the southern Emerjant coast. Huge chunks of farmland are being lost to the South Placidic Sea. Storms of unprecedented strength lashed a number of coastal cities this past winter. In short, the cost of joining the WPCC and adhering to the 40/40 Plan are high, but the likely cost of not doing so is even higher. Emerjant will earn 3 points for this objective if it and the other seven states in Politica sign the WPCC and each allocates the necessary factors to the 40/40 Plan.

Petropol

It is the industrialized countries of the world that are responsible for the horrible effects of global climate change. Without a doubt, Petropol is worried about the future of its environment; desertification continues to eat up much of the previously arable land in Petropol. In the east, Lake Irfan is in danger of drying up. But Petropol should not have to pay for the sins of others. In order to achieve this 3 point objective, Petropol must sign the WPCC but convince one or more states to absorb the 150 factor cost of getting Petropol to adhere to the 40/40 Plan.

Paxony

Paxons are aware that their early economic growth has sent millions of tons of carbon into the Politican atmosphere. To be consistent with their other priorities of global stability, economic cooperation, and collective justice, Paxony is ready to sign the WPCC and allocate the 450 factors it needs to in order to meet the standards of the 40/40 Plan. In fact, Paxony is even willing to help other states with factors if they agree to sign the WPCC. In order to achieve this 1 point objective, Paxony must sign the WPCC and allocate more than 450 factors to ensure both its and others' adherence to the 40/40 Plan.

Minerite

Evidence from the Drama Mountains has brought the reality of climate change all the way to the leadership offices in the Minerite capitol building in Mamalode. Minerite is a growing, industrial economy. It certainly shoulders the blame for contributing to the massive carbon emissions that have supposedly brought about this change. In order to earn 1 point for this objective, Minerite must sign the WPCC and allocate 450 factors toward adherence to the 40/40 Plan.

Scenario Outcome Assessment

*Use this space to answer the question your instructor
has provided for this scenario*

Diplomatic Notes

Country Action Report

■ Relevant Countries (list all that are involved in action):

1.   5.

2.   6.

3.   7.

4.   8.

■ Nature of Action (what are these countries agreeing to do?):

■ Required Signatures (majority, including CDM, for democracies; CDM only for others):

	CDM	DIP	ECA	INT	OPP
Paxony					
Refugia					
Emerjant					
Tundristan					
Industrael					
Islandia					
Petropol					
Minerite					

Instructor's Guide

While the IRiA handbook contains all the information you will need in order to successfully use the simulation in your course, this short appendix contains additional advice that will enable the whole exercise to run as smoothly as possible. If you have questions that are not answered here please visit http://tessman.myweb.uga.edu for an extensive set of responses to frequently asked questions and other resources.

Scheduling the Simulation

The IRiA Simulation can be integrated into your syllabus in a number of ways. The exercise is turn based, but the length and content of each turn is up to you. There are twelve simulation scenarios, so one way to organize the exercise is to have each scenario comprise one simulation turn. On the semester schedule, such a twelve-turn structure works quite well with each turn lasting one week. I have had success reserving one class meeting per week over the course of twelve weeks for the IRiA Simulation.

As an alternative, the simulation can be run continuously over a certain number of course meetings. If you decide on this option, I recommend no fewer than three consecutive meetings and no more than nine. You will not be able to devote an entire meeting to each scenario, but it is possible to organize the scenarios in other ways. If, for example, you choose to allocate three meetings to the simulation, you could devote one turn to each of the three groups of scenarios (international security, international political economy, and international organization). A third strategy for organizing the simulation is to allow the students to work on any of the twelve scenarios at any point during the simulation. It is still necessary to have a specified number of turns, but with this option you will no longer have turns that directly correlate with a specific scenario or group of scenarios. In my experience, this results in a more complex exercise, with more potential for compromise, coordination, and issue linkage. If you choose to use this option, I recommend setting aside anywhere from four to six course meetings solely for the simulation exercise.

Of course, it is very possible to run the entire IRiA Simulation outside of the classroom. Using phone, e-mail, and instant messenger, students can conduct formal diplomatic interactions, trade, and declare war in much the same way they would if in class. You and your students can access an electronic version of the country action forms (found at http://tessman.myweb.uga.edu) that can be e-mailed to you in lieu of a hard copy. The only challenge is to set a timetable that clearly delineates when certain turns begin and end. This is crucial to maintaining aspects of the simulation such as resource factor changes, trade, and declarations of war. Choosing this method for organizing the simulation reduces the class time devoted to the exercise, but it also eliminates the personal diplomatic interaction that students definitely thrive off of. No matter what option you choose, remember that the IRiA Simulation is flexible. As long as you retain the turn-based structure, the exercise will function as it is designed to.

Assigning Country and Individual Roles

Just as the simulation can be customized based on your scheduling needs, it is also suitable for courses of varying size. To function effectively, the IRiA Simulation requires a minimum of eight students (one student per country). While there is no absolute maximum number of students that can take part in the exercise, certain aspects of personal interaction and team cohesiveness are lost as the number of participating students exceeds fifty. With this in mind, the simulation is perfect for teaching assistants to use in the discussion sections that often accompany very large lecture courses. It is also very well suited for very small (at least eight students) to mid-sized (about fifty students) international relations courses of varying emphases.

In order to customize the IRiA Simulation to your particular class size, you must find a way to assign individuals to countries and individual governmental roles. This can be done in three ways: randomly, alphabetically, or by consideration. Either of the first two strategies is usually suitable, but if you have a special set of students or class needs, you may want to assign teams and roles according to your own rationale. In some cases, for example, I have assigned students to teams but then allowed them to negotiate and select governmental roles on their own.

Guidelines for Country and Role Assignments

Roles	Class Size				
	8–15	16–23	24–31	32–39	40–48
Chief decisionmaker	Yes	Yes	Yes	Yes	Yes
Diplomat	Some[a]	Yes	Yes	Yes	Yes (2)[b]
Economic adviser	No	Some[a]	Yes	Yes	Yes
Intelligence officer	No	No	Some[a]	Yes	Yes
Opposition leader	No	No	No	Some[a]	Yes

Notes: a. Certain countries will have this role filled, others will not. Add positions to democracies first (alphabetically) and then nondemocracies (alphabetically).

b. If all countries have all roles filled, assign additional students the role of co-diplomat. These students will share work with existing DIPs, but any and all DIPs have an independent vote when it comes to supporting policy actions submitted on country action forms.

The above table outlines some guidelines for customizing the IRiA Simulation to your specific class size. Every effort should be made to ensure that there are a roughly equal number of students representing each country. Positions should be filled one at a time for all countries before adding new positions for any country. For example, all CDM positions should be filled before any DIPs are assigned. If this rule is followed, there will never be more than a one-student difference between countries in the simulation. Positions should be filled in the following order: CDM, DIP, ECA, INT, and OPP. To reflect more diffuse policymaking, democracies (Islandia, Minerite, Paxony, and Refugia) should always have new positions added first.

| Declarations of War

In many cases, you will not encounter any declarations of war during the IRiA Simulation. In the event that conflict does arise, however, timing is everything. You need to be absolutely clear about deadlines for declaring war and responding to declarations. It should also be well understood that once a declaration of war is made, it cannot be altered; all aggressors are committed to the conflict and the guns factors that they have allocated are unchangeable. Likewise, once a response is made, all defenders are committed along with the guns factors they have allocated to defense.

Declarations of war must be made by a certain deadline *before* the end of the turn. These declarations must include all aggressor states, their targets, war aims, and the number of factors they are devoting to the war (this total will remain confidential until the target state(s) submit their response form at the end of the turn). The deadline for declarations of war is—like most aspects of the simulation—flexible. As long as you are clear about the deadlines and content required for any declarations of war, there are a number of options available to you. If you have organized the simulation around one-week (Monday–Friday) turns, the deadline for declarations could be Thursday afternoon and the response could be due at the end of the turn (Friday afternoon). If turns take place in a single course meeting, the deadline for declarations should be about 20 minutes before the end of the meeting and the deadline for response should be the end of the meeting. This second option results in some frantic negotiating and decisionmaking, but that is a valuable lesson about international crises in itself.

Information Summary/Newsletter

Depending on the manner in which you choose to organize the IRiA Simulation, it may also be helpful to send students a brief summary of events after each turn. If you have debriefing discussions in class after each turn, then it may not be necessary to create a hard copy of this summary. A short newsletter can be a very helpful "official record" of events, however, if you conduct the simulation outside of class or do not have sufficient time for debriefing discussions. The newsletter can also be used as a way to keep track of objective points, factor changes, and the outcomes of any declarations of war. At the IRiA website (http://tessman.myweb.uga.edu) you can find a number of newsletter templates available for use. You can also view sample newsletters that students have found helpful in recent years.

Assessment Questions

The website also provides an extensive (and frequently updated) list of assessment questions that help students link their experiences in the simulation to the relevant international relations theories, concepts, and issues you are addressing in class. You can use these assessment questions as a method of formal examination or simply as a required assignment. Students can write their response to the question you select in the space provided at the end of each scenario.

For Additional Information

This appendix addresses some of the important issues that you will encounter as you use the IRiA Simulation in your course. Perhaps the biggest asset of the simulation is its flexibility. As you become more familiar with it over time, you will discover new ways to optimize the IRiA Simulation for your particular needs. In the meantime, if you have any additional questions, please feel free to consult the extensive resources available online at http://tessman.myweb.uga.edu. Congratulations on making a great choice for your course. Enjoy the International Relations in Action Simulation!

About the Book

This hands-on exercise allows students to relate the concepts and issues at the foundation of global politics to the realities of international politics today.

As influential leaders in the fictional world of Politica, each team of students governs a country with a unique history, geography, and culture. The teams must use strategy and negotiation to succeed—and survive—seeking to achieve specific territorial, security, and economic objectives. In the process, they grapple with a range of complex challenges: energy, security, ethnic conflict, humanitarian intervention, environmental disaster, terrorism, nuclear proliferation, and more. Students also pursue individual objectives based on the governmental post they hold—and quickly learn that self-interest and national interest are not always compatible.

Teams are judged on their effectiveness in meeting stated objectives, but must also relate their practical experience to the academic content of the course. Toward this end, the book provides summaries, analysis, study questions, and additional sources of information for each of the theories and issues encountered during the simulation. Guidelines for instructors are also included.

International Relations in Action has been tested in multiple courses of various sizes, with students and instructors unanimously agreeing that it makes abstract theories practical and accessible, evokes an appreciation for the complexity of international politics, and generates enthusiasm for the study of international relations. In the representative words of one student, "It was the best learning experience I've ever had."

Brock F. Tessman is assistant professor of international affairs at the University of Georgia's School of Public and International Affairs.

International Relations
in Action